The Art of Creative Living

GARDEN OF GRACE

THE ART OF
CREATIVE LIVING

Making Every Day a Radiant Masterpiece

THOMAS KINKADE
AND PAM PROCTOR

WARNER
Faith®

NEW YORK   BOSTON   NASHVILLE

Scriptures noted RSV are taken from the REVISED STANDARD VERSION of
the Bible. Copyright © 1949, 1952, 1971, 1973 by the Division of Christian Education of
the National Council of the Churches of Christ in the U.S.A. Used by permission.

Scriptures noted NKJV are taken from THE NEW KING JAMES VERSION.
Copyright © 1979, 1980, 1982, Thomas Nelson, Inc., Publishers.

"How Great Thou Art" (pages 233–234) copyright © 1953 S.K. Hine. Assigned to Manna
Music, Inc., 35255 Brooten Road, Pacific City, OR 97135. Renewed 1981 by Manna
Music, Inc. All rights reserved. Used by permission. (ASCAP)

Warner Faith

Time Warner Book Group
1271 Avenue of the Americas, New York, NY 10020

Visit our Web site at www.twbookmark.com.

The Warner Faith name and logo are registered trademarks of the
Time Warner Book Group.

Book design by Fearn Cutler de Vicq
Printed in the United States of America
First Warner Books printing: April 2005
10 9 8 7 6 5 4 3 2 1

Library of Congress Cataloging-in-Publication Data

Kinkade, Thomas, 1958–
The art of creative living : making every day a radiant masterpiece / Thomas Kinkade.
p. cm.
Summary: "Artist Thomas Kinkade reveals how the creative process can provide a path to
greater spiritual awareness"—Provided by the publisher.
Includes bibliographical references.
ISBN 0-446-53234-7
1. Creativity—Religious aspects—Christianity. 2. Painting. 3. Christian life. I. Title.
BT709.5.K56 2005
248.4—dc 22   2004026448

*Dedicated to the memory of Charlie Bell,
a man who lived a creative life*

Contents

Contents

Contents

THE SIXTH DAY OF CREATIVE LIVING

The Cauldron of Conflict 183

THE SEVENTH DAY OF CREATIVE LIVING

The Spirit of Worship 213

CONCLUSION

Behold, a New Thing 245

Acknowledgments

Although the spark of creativity lies in each one of us, turning that creativity into a tangible, artistic product—whether it's a painting or a book—takes a special kind of synergy.

In the case of *The Art of Creative Living,* the synergy started with a happy reunion of three friends: Rolf Zettersten, Warner Books, and me. Rolf, who is publisher of Warner Faith, has been a good friend for more than fifteen years. During that time, we have developed not only a close personal bond but also a deep respect for one another professionally. A few years back, it was Rolf who introduced me to Warner Books, which published one of my first inspirational books for the general public. Then, two years ago, Rolf invited me to join Warner again for a new venture that he was spearheading, and *The Art of Creative Living* was born. To nurture the project through to completion, Rolf tapped a talented editor, Steve Wilburn.

I realized right from the start that in order to capture on paper the concepts and stories that were floating around in my head, I needed help. I am an artist, and if I am to fulfill my personal creative vision, it's imperative for me to stick to my day job—focused solely on the latest painting I'm working on in my studio. Fortunately, Warner introduced me to a new friend, Pam Proctor, a writer whose inspirational touch enlivened and expanded my own vision in *The Art of Creative Living.*

But the synergy didn't stop there. Behind the scenes, there were dozens of creative people striving to help me produce a superior work. First and foremost among them was my personal assistant, Denise Sanders, who is manager of Thomas Kinkade Studios—IvyGate. As the book was coming to fruition, Denise saw to it that I stayed happily on task, juggling my paintings, business deals, and this book.

Finally, no Thomas Kinkade project could be accomplished without the support of my most important editor and adviser, my wife, Nanette. Her constancy has given me the ultimate freedom to create without restraint. She has always understood the true secret to creativity: that in order to experience *The Art of Creative Living* to the fullest, each one of us needs affirmation and love.

Remember not the former things,
    nor consider the things of old.
Behold, I am doing a new thing;
    now it springs forth, do you not perceive it?

—Isaiah 43:18–19 RSV

America's Pride

A God of New Beginnings

Do you ever wonder how an artist does what he does? Do you ask yourself how he can take a blank canvas, and with just a few humble tools—a brush and some paint—infuse it with such life that when we see it, our faces brighten and a smile of recognition crosses our lips?

On the canvas touched by a gifted artist's hand, we see something familiar—something we remember in Grandma's house, on a vacation in the mountains, or during that business trip to a city on the East Coast. We see images of sunflowers dancing in a field . . . of cable cars straining up a hillside . . . of a man fishing in the Tetons . . . or of a Victorian house set amid a garden of roses.

It seems almost miraculous. How did the artist achieve such effects? How was he able to go from nothingness to a visual image so magnificent it takes our breath away? How was he able to create?

Of course, I could tell you the practical steps: how the artist sketches in the layout, masses in the forms, and adds bold blocks of color to create depth, shadow, and light. I could describe how he fine-tunes the image with small payoff details that turn a rounded form into a eucalyptus tree, or an oblong into a foreground bush, or a triangular shape into a distant mountain.

But that information would give you only part of the story. It wouldn't tell you what you really want to know, what you *need* to know: namely, that before even picking up his brush or putting the first dabs of color on the canvas, the artist first has to believe.

He has to believe that he can create. Even if his child is sick, his telephone bill is due, his wife is stressed out, or his dishwasher leaks, he has to *know* that he has the power within him to produce something wonderful. When he awakens each morning, he has to believe that although he might not be able to solve all his problems at once, he has the innate strength to deal alone with that blank canvas. He has to feel deep assurance that for an hour, a morning, or a day, he can create a world of beauty and hope and love, a world that reflects the vision that has been placed within his heart.

So the art of creation is an act of faith. It's a belief that we can take nothing more than a lump of clay or a chunk of stone and shape it into something magnificent. It's an understanding that within us, we have the power to take the crude, humble circumstances of our lives and ennoble them through creativity.

But this potential is not limited to the fine artist or the "pro" who makes a living from his creativity. Each of us possesses the creative spark, the innate ability to take whatever life bestows—pain or fear, courage or joy, heartbreak or disappointment—and transform it into a masterpiece. Every day is a blank canvas, waiting to be filled by *your* creative touch.

"But I'm not creative!" you might protest. "I just don't have it in me."

But you're wrong. The creative impulse is fundamental to human nature, a basic instinct as powerful as our primeval drive to survive or reproduce. More often than not, though, we have buried it under the burdens of our lives. We have consumed ourselves with busywork, anxieties, and priorities of the moment, rather than with the calling of the eternal—the calling of God.

From the beginning of space and time, creativity has been at the center of God's purpose for you and me. It seems significant that the first image of God portrayed in the ancient Scriptures was as Creator: "In the beginning God created . . ."

As this early story of the earth and heavens unfolds, God emerges as the Master Artist with infinite skill and imagination who, in a series of bold strokes, first fills the canvas of reality with light . . . next, with a rather mysterious "firmament" or "expanse" or "dome" . . . then, with dry land, vegetation, birds and sea creatures, beasts of the earth . . . and finally, humankind.

Like the act of creation itself, your life is an ongoing creative act, driven by bursts of divine imagination that empower you to invent, inspire, motivate, and envision. Every day, you are called to exercise the creativity that is your birthright.

But how do you start? How do you cut through the dishes and the phone ringing and your boss bearing down on you and the baby crying to ignite the creative spark within you? How do you find your creative purpose when you've never had an inclination to paint, or to compose, or to write, or to dance?

Let me make a suggestion: Open your inner eye right now to that blank canvas that is the rest of your life. What do you most yearn to do? What would give you the most satisfaction or enjoyment? What is your dream job, or your ideal relationship, or your perfect day? What is the creative vision you have for your life?

Is it to run a company, or bring harmony to your family, or bring romance back into your marriage? Is it to take salsa lessons, or walk the beach, or fix up that room that has been bugging you for years?

Chances are, whatever your dreams, whatever your secret longings, you haven't thought about them for a long, long time, because down deep, you don't believe they can be realized. In short, you don't believe you can create. You don't wake up believing like an artist that you can take the blank canvas of your day and create the world as you want it to be.

Yet each of us has the power. As he formed us in the womb, God placed eternity in our hearts, so that we would be restless, uncomfortable, and unfulfilled until we had connected with our divinely ordained calling—until we had lit the creative spark within.

Of course, you can choose to suppress your creative inner yearnings and never pick up the tools that will allow you to create. You can cover your canvas in unrelieved darkness and layers of fear, anxiety, or gloom. You can allow yourself to be overwhelmed by challenges or problems that you perceive as great personal threats or obstacles.

On the other hand, you can approach your creative potential with more expectant eyes. You can see it as a wonderful opportunity, a priceless gift. You can open your mind to the possibility that each day—whether you're a lawyer, a full-time mom, a plumber, a volunteer, or a computer whiz—you have the potential to create a radiant new masterpiece.

The creative impulse is not a onetime phenomenon; rather, it is an ongoing part of the complete human experience. Every day is a new day, a new canvas. Whatever you did or failed to do yesterday can be repaired or changed today. Wherever your life has taken you—whether through a divorce, a financial crisis, a devastating illness, or a disappointment at work—you can start again. God is not just the original Creator and Master Artist, but also the God of new beginnings. His mercies never come to an end; they are new every morning.

So your blank canvas stands ready. Will you pick up the brush with me? Today? Right now? Will you dare to dream?

In my paintings, I try to touch you personally. I try to draw you into each scene so that you can share my dreams and my emotions. I want you to wander with a sense of wonderment through majestic landscapes and, in flights of imagination, open cottage doors and bask in the warmth of inner light.

Now, I invite you to take the next step. On the following pages, I will lead you into my canvas, into the world of Thomas Kinkade. Once inside, you'll join me for seven "days" of creative experience and celebration. It is my hope that as you witness the unfolding of God's creative vision, you will be inspired to see and believe in your own calling, a divine summons to live every day creatively and turn your life into an exciting work of art.

How will you design your personal canvas? What will be your first creative line, sketch, or brushstroke? The choice is in your hands.

Light the spark. Approach every decision you make, every word you speak, every task you undertake, every challenge you confront, as a brand-new brushstroke in the art of creation. If you do, I promise that you'll bask in an eternal glow that just might transform your life.

The Art of Creative Living

THE FIRST DAY
OF CREATIVE LIVING

The Art of Solitude

Solitude is the audience-chamber of God.

— WALTER SAVAGE LANDOR

PATHWAY TO PARADISE

Eternity in Your Heart

All true creativity—in relationships, business, spirituality, or the arts—begins at some tranquil center deep inside your being. You can't really create unless you have first discovered and explored that quiet inner dimension.

So your first challenge in learning the art of creation in your life is to *find* that special inner place, where all your greatest dreams and deepest personal beliefs reside. Then, you'll want to contemplate and enjoy that sanctuary of personal solitude for a time until, finally, you're in a position to ignite your passion and reach out to change the world around you.

But understand, I'm not talking about some abstract point of philosophy here. This is a supremely practical truth. Think about yourself for a moment. If you're honest, you probably will find, as you look deep inside, that you harbor a burning desire: You want to retreat from the pressures of life into a special place where you can feel totally at peace just being alone with your reflections and dreams. We all want to hole up in such an inviolate place on occasion. I know I do. But first, of course, you have to find it.

And by the way, this place I'm talking about isn't necessarily linked to a physical location. Rather, it's a sacred space in the depths of your being—in your spirit and your heart—where your creative impulses are most likely to have free rein. You know intuitively that when you are firmly ensconced in this private realm, your greatest potential can finally be realized. And ultimately, you can become the person you were really meant to be.

It isn't that you don't love interacting with your family and friends, or operating as a productive and useful member of society. But you know that to be a truly creative person, you desperately need a place apart, a hidden corner where you can listen to that certain, singular voice in your heart.

In fact, if you don't first enter this place, which above all is a state of mind and being, there is little chance that you will ignite your passion and be swept along in a great flow of creativity. So the stable, fertile space inside comes first. Then you will have a platform—a platform rooted in eternal concerns—on which to consider the specific nature of your creative impulses and practical ways you might realize them.

Although finding your special inner space might seem a rather complex or difficult assignment, the path to the destination may actually lie in plain view. Let me illustrate by introducing you to Sylvia, who works behind the counter at a fast-food restaurant in Cuthbert, Georgia.

I learned about Sylvia through a friend of mine, who happened to be carrying a copy of one of my books when she walked up to the counter to place her order. She had just laid the book on the counter and was fumbling with her purse when Sylvia, the young African-American woman at the cash register, spied my name on the book cover.

"Thomas Kinkade!" the young woman exclaimed. "I have one of his cottages. I bought it in Germany."

My friend did a double take because she had never run into anyone who had purchased Kinkade real estate in Germany. In fact, she had never heard of any such thing.

Soon the mystery solved itself when Sylvia explained that while she was browsing through a military post-exchange gift shop while her husband was stationed in Germany, a little porcelain cottage on one of the shelves caught her eye. Somehow, the replica infused her with an inexplicable sense of tranquillity and almost immediately seemed to free her mind to range over her most profound dreams and aspirations.

As it happened, that little cottage, which now has a permanent spot on a bureau in Sylvia's home in Cuthbert, was a reproduction of one of the cozy country hideaways in my paintings. In the ensuing conversation, it quickly became apparent that Sylvia had never read any of my books or even seen any of my paintings. But for some reason, when she focused on that small cottage or cradled it in her hands, she found she was transported to another dimension.

"Every time I look at that cottage—or even think about it—I'm reminded that somewhere there's a place I can be all by myself, peaceful and quiet," said Sylvia, her eyes twinkling at the thought.

With that, she turned back to the French-fry machine, hustling to fill my friend's order. A few minutes later, Sylvia returned with the fries and a smile so bright and serene that for a moment my friend thought she had become a valued patron of the most elegant restaurant imaginable.

Clearly, Sylvia had discovered the secret to finding creative solitude in the midst of her busy day. As she recalled a simple cottage filled with light—a light that seemed to cast a warming glow on her own life—her mood, imagination, and sensitivity to others soared. Sylvia succeeded in finding a supremely quiet and tranquil inner dimension, a piece of eternity in her heart that extended quite naturally into her surroundings and relationships.

I don't know whether Sylvia's special glow that day lasted for just a moment or for hours on end. But I do know that my friend's life benefited significantly from that young woman's potent creative touch. It's hard not to be moved, and transformed just a little bit for the better, when we encounter the power of another person's quiet and profound inner solitude.

THE HOUR OF PRAYER

Merging with the Mind of God

After you discover a path that leads to a quiet clearing deep inside your heart—and then step into the space with the intention of contemplating and expressing your own creativity—you will soon realize that further preparation is necessary. Almost immediately, if you're like most other people I know, you'll find yourself asking a couple of disconcerting questions:

"Am I *really alone* as I become more 'centered' here in this creative inner space? And if I'm not, who or what else is present with me?"

The search for true, empowering solitude—that intangible place where eternity resides and inspires—prompts such questions. Even more unsettling, coming face-to-face with our creative aspirations and goals often releases feelings of *loneliness*—destructive, oppressive feelings of cut-off seclusion that can completely immobilize the imagination. In my own creative work, I have found that a prerequisite for inspired creativity is the ability to ward off the paralysis of loneliness by understanding that *I am never really alone.*

For sustained creative output, we all need some sort of reassuring, comforting, confidence-inspiring presence to sustain us during the dry periods and the hard going. Some may visualize this presence as a kind of congenial companion. Others may imagine they can feel the steady, strong hand of a diligent collaborator guiding their brush or pen this way and that. Still others may assume that near at hand, there's a chorus of nebulous, invisible encouragers to whom they can talk or mutter.

What's the identity of this other presence in *your* life? Your inner trek toward the creative life may not have carried you quite far enough to say. But if pressed, you might speculate that it's just possible you've been joined by some comfortable alter ego, or a personal artistic muse, or an undefined spiritual presence, . . . or God.

So go ahead and probe deeper into your heart, the seat of your very being. Search with great care for the centered orientation from which you can begin to create. But at the same time, engage your mind and spirit in an "inner conversation" with questions like these:

> — *If I'm not really alone, then who might be with me?*
> — *As I begin to dream and create, what force will sustain and inspire me?*
> — *Who will give me extra strength in hard times, when finances are low, time is short, or creativity seems to have shut down?*

I know that when I ask myself such questions, a quick, sure answer comes to mind: Even though I may *seem* to be alone, I'm really partnering with God in the creative act—whether I'm aware of his presence or not. Furthermore, I firmly believe that as I draw closer to that spot inside me where my maximum creativity can burst forth, I am actually beginning to *merge* with the mind of God.

Now, don't roll your eyes. I'm not talking about some form of pantheism, where God is equated with all the laws and matter in the universe. To the contrary, I know that God is my Creator, not just an extension of myself. I'm convinced that he is the Master Artist, who has an infinite existence *outside* my mind and body; he is the separate Person who bestowed on me the talents and gifts I possess.

But at the same time, as I draw nearer to the heart of true creativity, I perceive that there is, paradoxically, an increasing identity between God and me. I believe he wants to think, work, and create through me—and that means when I'm doing my best work on my paintings, I should expect to somehow become one with him.

On the other hand, you certainly don't have to be in a painter's studio, or any other physical location, to merge with the mind of God. Instead, you may find yourself bursting with creativity in a van surrounded by kids and dogs and turtles and Grandma (as I often am). Or you might end up doing your best work on a busy street with crowds of passersby on Fifth Avenue in New York City. (I've found my creative place there as well.)

Suppose you're working in customer service at Sears, or playing softball with the guys on Saturdays, or running the PTA meeting, or coaching peewee football. In all those ordinary situations, you have the opportunity to be supremely creative—to "max out" with your imagination in the most mundane of settings. But first, it's necessary to find a profound inner place of quiet and solitude.

I'm reminded of one female employee in a large clothing store who had to spend all day, every day, for weeks before the Christmas holidays handling complaints. For the first few days, she became frustrated, angry, and thoroughly strung out by the end of her shift.

Then, one evening she retreated into her deepest being—into some hidden place in her psyche—and had a heart-to-heart with herself:

You can't keep this up—you know that, don't you? Another week of this, and you'll have a breakdown. And it's still three weeks before Christmas. So what are you going to do?

She paused and found herself listening—for what or whom, she wasn't sure. There was no voice, but somehow she began to feel a little calmer. Then she continued her dialogue with herself.

Okay, you could quit. But you need the money—and besides, you're not a quitter. So if you stay, how are you going to change things at that complaint counter? It says Customer Service, but you and everybody else know you're just there to handle complaints. How can you make that situation pleasant—or at least bearable?

Then she smiled. The absurdity of her predicament hit her all at once, and she realized that the answer was to bring a little holiday cheer into the complaint department, where the natural tendency was to be at one another's throat.

In a nutshell, she came up with a multifaceted creative solution for her dilemma. First of all, she drew up a little sign, which she planned to place prominently on her counter: "Every Problem Is a Blessing in Disguise."

Then, after thinking about the typical complaints and problems that were presented to her every day, she began to categorize them on a pad of paper. Overall, there seemed to be eight main categories, such as, "This product is defective—and I want my money back."

She then scribbled down her possible responses to the annoyed or discouraged customers—words that might elicit a smile or, better yet, put them on a path to a product they might really like.

The next day, she began to implement her ideas and was amazed at how her change in attitude transformed her work atmosphere. All of a sudden, she was seeing more smiles and receiving more "thank you"s in one hour than she had witnessed before in an entire day.

For the first time in memory, this woman actually enjoyed the holidays, despite her challenging job. Also, as she reflected on her experience after the season was over, she realized that the secret to her success lay in that quiet time she had spent in her living room. During that brief period of solitude, she had allowed her imagination to roam free—and lead her to solutions that otherwise would have remained out of reach.

I've never worked behind a complaint counter, but I have been in similar difficult, irritating situations as I try to solve problems in my painting or related business ventures. Also, much like this woman, I may sit quietly and ruminate on my situation and toss out questions to another presence in the room with me.

The customer service employee might say she was talking to her alter ego. I'd say that my questions are more in the nature of prayers—overtures to the Spirit of God, whom I sense hovering palpably at my elbow. In whatever physical or social circumstances I find myself, my creative potential always depends directly on how I'm getting along with God at that particular moment. The more my inner self conforms to his will, the more my creative mind merges with his mind.

When that closeness occurs—and as I continue to toss out comments and questions about my situation—I often sense my thoughts moving in new directions. Sometimes, I even think I can hear a whisper that's nudging me in a specific direction and summoning me to unleash all my talents and do my best with the pending task. In those moments, I know that my best creative work may be near at hand. Or as the great devotional writer Oswald Chambers put it while working at his high-stress chaplain's outpost in Egypt during World War I, I may be poised to achieve "my utmost for his highest."

So now your creative journey inward has begun, and you're moving into the most fertile, creative fields of your mind and spirit. Your creative expectations have been aroused, and your imagination has come into sharper focus. Perhaps you really have caught a glimpse of what it means to have "eternity in your heart" and to begin to "merge with the mind of God." In any event, you understand that you need solitude, and not just the solitude of loneliness. Rather, for maximum creativity, you require an inner space filled and controlled by a positive presence outside yourself—a Spirit, if you will, who can comfort, direct, and advise.

But in practical terms, what's the first step you should take to ensure that every day will be a creative day? For me, that first step occurs before I even take a physical step, in those half-waking moments just before I arise each morning.

GLORY OF MORNING

First Contact

I've discovered that most creative people get started early. If you begin your morning in a kind of *dynamic* solitude, with a stimulated, free-ranging state of mind, you'll likely remain in that imaginative mode as the day wears on.

How do I make my first contact with creativity in the morning? Over the years, I've found it's important for me just to lie there in bed immediately after I wake up and turn a Bible passage over and over in my mind. A phrase or sentence like "The Lord is my strength" says it all for me. Or maybe I'll dwell on "The Lord is my shepherd."

I don't strain to remember huge blocks of Scripture. This is not a time for deep theological study. Just a snippet or two from some familiar passage will do. A few minutes of dwelling on one or several such passages gives me a sense of active engagement with the eternal presence in my life—the presence whose creativity is boundless and who assures me as I work, "All things are indeed possible."

Maybe other types of literature are more likely to turn on your imagination and motivation. For example, some people get "juiced up" creatively by focusing for a while in the morning on some pithy saying or inspiring line of poetry. That's one of the reasons I included at the beginning of this section that provocative line from Walter Savage Landor: "Solitude is the audience-chamber of God."

Another line that can work as a meditation on creativity is this observation by Henry David Thoreau: "I never found the companion that was so companionable as solitude." Or you might be drawn to an insight by

James Russell Lowell: "Solitude is as needful to the imagination as society is wholesome for the character."

On the other hand, maybe you're too sleepy or disoriented for poetry or Bible verses so early in the morning. First, you may have to get moving physically; then, your mind will be more likely to start working. I know many people who absolutely must engage in physical exercise the first thing in the morning before their cerebral faculties are able to kick in. So they take a walk or bike ride through the local park, or a jog along the beach.

For other people, gardening serves as an early morning outlet to stimulate the imagination. Just digging up a few clods of dirt or a bunch of weeds can cause the mind and spirit to move in more productive, imaginative directions.

I've had some of the best ideas for my painting while strolling alone down a quiet street or country path just after sunrise. When you're in the great outdoors, counting the stars, feeling the breeze, or observing the infinite variety of plants and animals, you can't help but find yourself face-to-face with the Author of creativity himself.

But let me emphasize: I think it's important to make your first contact with creativity as early as possible in the day. If you put off this initial time of focus and reflection, your imaginative powers won't be likely to engage until the day is well under way.

After you've made your first contact, you will most likely find that you need additional creative boosts at other points in the day, especially if you're working long, intense hours on a project. In other words, it may be helpful, in effect, to start the day all over again with a second or even a third time of meditation, a walk, or some other relaxing, diverting activity. With such creative breaks at midday, you'll be better prepared to finish the day in a surge of productivity.

I myself need more than one "first contact" during especially demanding days. So I usually set aside time on a private sundeck near my painting area every noontime to commune with God about my work and my ideas. To facilitate this "divine meeting," I've rigged up a wooden stand for my Bible, complete with a drawer for notebooks and writing tools. As I sit basking in the warm sunshine with the blue sky overhead, I often lose myself in the awesome power of creation. In that tranquil setting, I imagine myself in some heavenly garden, communing with the Creator. Such orchestrated daydreaming keeps me focused on the true source of my creative powers.

How does this first-contact approach work in practice? Let me give you a personal example from one of my recent projects—a "plein air" impressionistic painting I completed outdoors one sunny autumn morning. The setting was my hometown in northern California.

On Saturday morning I awoke with an almost uncontrollable urge to create. I could sense the electricity in the air.

This is the day which the Lord has made; let us rejoice and be glad in it, I thought to myself as I lay there in bed.

I repeated that verse from Psalm 118 over and over. Before long, the words took hold of my mind, and I could feel my will merging with a transcendent will beyond me. My heart opened to embrace the incredible possibilities God had in store for me. This particular day—my special creative day—would really be God's day, when he would direct the creative flow.

With the psalm still on my lips, I was primed to engage the canvas, the world, the entire cosmos—but my first act of creativity was much more mundane. My usual routine involves praying with my wife, Nanette, even before I climb out of bed. But that morning, Nanette was exhausted and wanted to sleep in. So instead of pressing my agenda on her, I chose to roll out quietly and leave her asleep on the one day a week when, as a mother of four, she has that luxury.

Taking one last glance down at her blonde head buried deep in the pillows, I tiptoed into the living room, where I spent some individual time in prayer. Then I peered out the window at the clear blue sky and felt an impulse to do something outrageous. I threw open the French doors, strode onto the backyard grass, and raised my hands in worship as a gesture of thankfulness for the glorious, cloudless day! My feet soon joined in the reverie, and I found myself jumping about in a dance of joy. It was a spontaneous creative act of worship—a personal celebration—just like King David's dance before the Lord in the Old Testament.

"Thank you, Lord!" I exclaimed under my breath, trying not to wake Nanette and the girls. "Hallelujah!"

Luckily my neighbors didn't look over the fence. If they had, they would have seen a normally self-controlled man twirling on the lawn like one of his grade-school children.

Still giddy with expectation after my time of impulsive worship, I packed the car with my art equipment and work apron and also threw in some water and granola bars as snacks. Then I made myself a pot of tea. Finally, I pulled on my jeans and an old blue plaid shirt, topped off my ensemble with a red-brimmed baseball cap, jumped into my car, and headed to the historic center of town.

Sitting behind the wheel of my convertible—a vintage 1950s model that I wanted to include in my painting—I basked in the warm breeze on my face. As I drove down the mountain toward town, I rehearsed my artistic strategy: "This painting needs to be dead-on target. It has to progress as strategically as a chess game."

But I didn't let those anxious thoughts overwhelm me. Instead, I confronted them head-on with a little prayerful self-talk: "This painting will be right, because God is at the center of it. He has opened the doors for this opportunity, and so I can turn the creative results over to God."

As a seasoned artist, I reminded myself that if I didn't get everything done that day, I could always go back and paint another day. I also knew that if I didn't like the results, I could rework it.

Such thoughts are reassuring to me. God is indeed a God of new beginnings. His mercy is fresh every morning. This morning—my morning for an entirely new painting—would be just another day of mercy.

I turned onto Main Street and prayed one of those quirky but faith-filled parking-space prayers: "Lord, please let there be space in front of Gilley's."

Gilley's, the old-time coffee shop where all the locals gather for breakfast, was right next to the theater. I needed a parking spot in front so that I could paint my old-fashioned car into the scene to help set a nostalgic mood. As it turned out, there was a car parked in just the *wrong* place, smack in front of Gilley's. But a few minutes after I had set up my easel and started to paint, the miraculous happened: The owner of the offending vehicle spontaneously approached me and offered to move.

That unexpected, gracious gesture reaffirmed for me that I was on the right track and in a genuine creative flow. Also, the man's offer reminded me that in the midst of creativity, I must always be open to serendipity, to that unexpected event or circumstance that could open new vistas in my imagination.

I knew I would need that kind of expansive attitude in order to manage the succession of people who would inevitably stop and chat. There's something about a street painter that attracts attention, whether he's working in a small, tucked-away village in the Austrian Alps, at a busy city intersection, or on a bluff overlooking the ocean in Monterey. When I work on location, it seems that every amateur artist or interested passerby will stop and interrupt, offering random comments or insights.

"Do you mind if I watch?" someone will say.

"Is this how you make your living?" another will quip.

"I can do better than that," a teenager might remark, thinking that she's out of earshot.

In order to keep my cool—and my creative focus—I reminded myself to keep perspective: "Remember, you're onstage every day of your life. Each of us in our own way is a walking, talking exhibit of God's love."

That particular plein air project unfolded smoothly, even though I constantly had to field questions from bystanders. Successful plein air painting often requires achieving a delicate creative balance between inner tranquillity and outward turmoil. The artist moves in and out, from an inner centeredness that begins first thing in the morning . . . to an interactive mode with the surrounding world . . . and then back again to be nurtured in centered solitude.

Yet most often, the day's experience begins with that first creative contact, just as morning dawns. But where—*physically*—should you expect your most creative activity to occur? For a possible answer, let's take a flight back in time.

STUDIO IN THE GARDEN

A Room of One's Own

I t should be evident by now that to be maximally creative, the most important prerequisite is finding your way to a state of inner solitude, a secure dimension of rest deep in your spirit or psyche that provides a firm platform for imaginative work.

But it's also true that we all need a *physical* location to which we can withdraw for much of our creativity. I usually recommend that before a person sits down for a serious creative effort, it's a good idea to identify and prepare a space of some sort, no matter how modest.

Sometimes, the choice of such a physical location is easy. You may have a spare bedroom or storage room you can convert to a "workspace." Or maybe you've got an attic that can be fixed up. On the other hand—especially if you're just starting out—you may have to settle for a corner of a little-used room, or a section of your garage, or even a closet. If you simply can't find a place at home, you could try the local library or a quiet corner of a coffee shop. The only real requirement is that the place be relatively quiet and subject to as little human traffic as possible.

Virginia Woolf had it right: To be creative, she said, all that is needed is a little money and "a room of one's own."

Of course, the "little money" part is always nice, but even without that, chances are you'll be able to find some solitary nook where you can let your creativity explode.

Ever since I was a child, I've known instinctively that I needed a room of my own to maximize my creativity. It wasn't so much that I wanted to be alone, although that was part of it. Rather, I wanted a place that I could dominate physically and psychologically, a space whose every corner I could fill with tools, books, and projects directed to one thing only: my creative life as an artist. I wanted a place where the minute I stepped inside, nothing stood between me and my act of creation.

When I was a kid, my brother and I shared a room, but my mother had this wonderful notion that as we approached our teens, we should have some privacy. As a hard-pressed single parent, she didn't have much money, but she never lacked the ability to think creatively about domestic arrangements. So after analyzing the potential for our fairly ample-sized room, she hired a carpenter friend to come in and build a wall right down the middle of our sleeping space.

My brother, Pat, and I ended up with two odd-shaped rooms about six or eight feet wide by fifteen feet long. The result wasn't too roomy, nor was it conventional. But at least we each had our own space. And Mom's renovation had put me in a position to do a little creative designing of my own.

After the privacy wall was installed, I decided to further enhance the arrangement by adding a sleeping loft, which left me with two feet or so between the bed and the ceiling. After crawling up there at bedtime, I felt not so much as though I was in a bed as in a cocoon, or perhaps in a confined sailor's hammock aboard a nineteenth-century sailing vessel.

Below decks, though, was where all my creative action took place. I put a chair and a bookshelf against one wall, where I could sit and read all my favorite art books. Also, I found an inexpensive wooden desk at a secondhand store, which I modified into a drawing table, with all my pencils, pens, paints, and brushes arranged neatly within its drawers. At that time, I was working mostly in charcoal, pen, and ink, with some watercolor work. As the months and years went by, the space grew more crowded. I hung T squares and triangles; I mounted an electric pencil sharpener within easy reach on the makeshift ceiling; I built receptacles and racks to hold new tools and materials with which I was experimenting.

Despite the limitations, that modest, confined little creative place was the scene of some of my most important early artistic discoveries. In that space, I discovered the secrets of light and shade, mastered the art of ink cross-hatching, rendered figures with foreshortening, and learned to blend tones and soften edges. Every discovery released new ideas and feelings of exhilaration. And it all happened in that tiny little room, barely the size of many walk-in closets.

But that was just the beginning of my personal workspace saga. Ever since I was a small child, one of my favorite books had been a volume written by Arthur Guptill titled *Norman Rockwell Illustrator*. (See the "Selected References" section at the back of this book.) In addition to Rockwell's artwork, the book contained detailed pictures and descriptions of his studio—which started me dreaming about what my own studio might look like some day. So even as I was furnishing and fine-tuning my small space just under that loft, I was building larger, more luxurious quarters in my mind.

Before long, I set my sights on our family's unused laundry room, an eight-by-ten-foot space with electrical outlets intended for a washer and dryer. Since Mom couldn't afford a washer or dryer, our family, like many families of limited means, relied on the local dime Laundromat.

By most measures, the average person looking for a workplace wouldn't have considered that laundry room. But to me, it began to beckon like a palatial studio appointed by a patron of Michelangelo. Certainly, it was always kind of moldy in there and a peculiar smell always lingered from the gas heater, which made the space way too warm, if not sweltering during the summer. But I managed to convince my mom that with the addition of a few simple shelves, and with some reorganization, the laundry room could become a first-rate studio for an up-and-coming artist. Finally, I had a sizable private space, a whole room that was not at all a bad deal for an impecunious teenager.

The first thing I did was to move in plenty of oil paints so that before long, the place actually started to smell more like an artist's studio than a gas-tainted laundry room. With this step up in the quality and size of my creative space, my development as a young artist accelerated. Oils now became my main métier and have continued to be the dominant medium in my art ever since.

Just as I began to become a little dissatisfied with the laundry-room milieu, I left home for college. Now, it seemed, I was back at square one in my studio search, but in a way, that move was a blessing in disguise. Free to improve on the laundry-room scene, I checked into my college dorm and immediately started scouring the neighborhood for a new creative space.

Needless to say, I didn't have much money to spend, but my studio hunt soon paid off. I found a storage room in the basement of a run-down apartment building and negotiated with the landlord to rent the space for $50 a month. At the time, that was a fortune to me, but now I had a twenty-by-twenty-foot room—a huge size increase over my mom's laundry room. Also, the place had an adequate seven-foot ceiling.

There were drawbacks, however. Unsightly pipes ran along the ceiling, and there were no windows. The space resembled a cave, but at least I had a fairly roomy space of my own where I could dream and create for the foreseeable future.

Step-by-step, I have enlarged and redesigned my creative space over the years until my studio is now a quaint freestanding cottage nestled in a grove of redwood trees just behind our family home. A four-thousand-volume collection of art and research books fills the oak-paneled library that adjoins the main painting atelier. A huge stone fireplace, modeled after the one in Yosemite's Ahwahnee Hotel, dominates one side of the main room, and twenty-five-foot ceilings preside over the expanse.

My current space also includes an office and a drafting room, not to mention the outdoor sundeck, where I retreat for quiet times of study and prayer.

Dozens of works in progress litter the entire landscape of my studio, serving as a kind of serial progress report on every one of my pending projects. I get ideas just wandering among them and communing with them.

Finally—and this is one of my most important requirements for a creative space—my studio space is sacrosanct. When I'm working, I let few people inside, and except for Nanette, my children, and a housekeeper who removes a layer of dust about once a month, I don't let anyone touch a thing. When I close the door behind me, I know I've entered a special, personal environment that I've designed in a way that's completely familiar, predictable, and conducive to my peculiar artistic needs. Nothing, but nothing, is allowed to stop the creative flow.

Throughout this studio saga, I became increasingly aware of how essential it was for me to experience inner solitude, even as I moved into better-equipped and larger quarters—and I would expect the same principle would apply to you. You may have access to the roomiest of quarters with the latest high-tech computer systems or whatever else you need to pursue your dreams. But if you lack that calm center that can't be measured in space and time, you'll never reach your full potential as a creative person.

Undoubtedly, you already have some ideas about how you want to design your ideal creative platform of inner and outer solitude. But let me offer a final suggestion about a few simple, practical steps that may be helpful as you proceed.

SWEETHEART GAZEBO

Designing Your Place of Solitude

No matter where you find yourself—in a prison cell, a tiny apartment, or a sprawling mansion—you are the recipient of an important gift. You actually possess *right now* the inner resources and physical surroundings necessary to launch some great, inspired work in your life.

But even though many people I know feel that they harbor a creative spark, they complain they can't get started because they lack the right place to do creative work. By now, I've heard most of the excuses:

- "My home isn't big enough."
- "My home is big enough, but it's dull and uninspiring."
- "My spouse or kids are always interrupting."
- "I can't work at home, and I can't afford an outside space."
- "I don't have time to design or plan the proper environment."
- "I have a place to work and think, but it's too cluttered—and I can't figure out how to put things in order."
- "I have a place, but it's too spare—and I can't afford the tools and supplies and furniture I need."
- "Somehow, I just can't seem to get organized!"

In fact, I've discovered over the years that the only thing really required in the way of physical space is not the perfect studio, but just an available place—which you have the will to occupy. I've painted on a portable easel standing in traffic on Market Street, typed a book proposal on a rented manual typewriter in a Times Square Burger King, and worked on final edits of this very manuscript while sitting in a quiet corner beside the pool during a family vacation in Hawaii.

So the first challenge as you design the physical setting for your solitude is to look at your physical circumstances, whatever they are, as an opportunity—as a platform provided by God for unique achievement. Then, use your creative ability to turn those circumstances to your advantage.

Erica—a single mother whose last child finally left for college—is an interesting example. At first, she found herself behaving as the classic "empty nester," always feeling at loose ends when she came home from work to an empty apartment. Her lack of a sense of purpose, coupled with mild depression, caused her to get behind with her usual volunteer work and cultural projects. In other words, the lack of family responsibilities, which you might think would have triggered a burst of new activity, actually immobilized her.

But then she decided the time had arrived to use her solitude, which had deteriorated into loneliness, to her advantage. Looking around, she saw that she had a great deal going for her, including a couple of empty rooms and no outside distractions unless she wanted them. As for purpose in life, she possessed a firm set of convictions about the importance of continuing to improve herself and also her responsibility to share her blessings with those less fortunate. Her main problem when the children were still at home was a lack of time to pursue these goals and values.

"So why not start doing some of the things I've always been waiting to do—such as pampering myself, reading more, and doing extra community work?" she told herself one night. "After all, life isn't a dress rehearsal. It's the real show."

Now, Erica has transformed her living room into the ultimate illustration of creative solitude. Every night when she arrives home from work, she lights a couple of candles for dinner and when the weather is cold enough, she sets a fire in the fireplace. Every evening meal is now an elegant event, which calms her mind and prepares her to think more expansively and creatively.

As her dinner is cooking, she often muses on the day's events and conversations and keeps a writing pad close at hand to write down ideas for her volunteer projects. Then, after her meal, she'll usually retire to the hot-pink chaise lounge in her bedroom to read and reflect.

In effect, Erica has found a way to combine inner and outward solitude in such a way that now, she never feels lonely. Instead, she has designed a physical platform that nurtures her spirit and often energizes her for her various projects the next day.

If you would like to find what Erica has found—a version of the creative personal space we have been discussing in these first few pages—I'd suggest this simple action plan:

Find Your Ideal Inner Space

Somehow, your special inner place of solitude must be connected to your worldview—the spiritual and philosophical values you consider most important. For me, the ultimate source for finding and developing such an inner space has been the ancient Scriptures, the Old and New Testaments. But it will be up to you to find the "center point" in your own way.

Find a Physical Space—but Feel Free to Start Small

You can, quite literally, transform almost any space into a place that will provide you a perfectly adequate platform to do your more creative thinking and work.

Do you lack an extra room? Then for starters, take a little four-by-four-foot rug—an old one that's preferably already a little dirty or stained—and lay it down in one corner of your living room. Or put it in a corner of your bedroom. But whatever you do, keep it well away from the TV.

Now, if your burning desire has been to paint, put an easel on that rug. Or you could set up a typewriter or computer if you're an aspiring writer, or just a simple pad of paper and a pencil.

Now put a chair on it.

Now put your palette and brushes or other necessary tools down on the rug.

There's your personal creative space. That's all you need. Now, it's time to start creating. Or just try thinking and dreaming!

Give Thanks for Your Spiritual and Physical Space

Your special place of solitude—defined by both your inward values and your chosen work area—is an essential "brushstroke" in your life if you hope to become truly adept at the art of creation.

So accept this current place of yours with thanksgiving. Above all, don't allow yourself to grouse, "I'll have to put up with this little room or corner now, but someday . . ."

Simply being thankful for what you currently have will unleash one of the most powerful spiritual forces in life. When I give thanks, my mood lifts and my mind opens to new possibilities. If, in less-than-perfect circumstances, I say, "Thanks, God—even though this may be the only creative space I'll ever have," I usually proceed immediately to make great creative strides. And that sets the stage for even greater accomplishments in the future.

Minimize Distractions

"I can't be creative—I have kids!" you may say.

So I say, "Wait a minute. Is there a lock on your bedroom door?"

If not—or if you have some other reason for not wanting to lock your kids out of your bedroom—find a closet or work when your kids are out playing or your spouse is doing errands. If you really want to create something, there are no good excuses.

Anh Vu Sawyer, for example, a mother of three, did most of the research and drafting for her Vietnam memoir, *Song of Saigon,* while sitting on the floor of a pantry in her home in Colorado Springs, with Wheaties and Cheerios boxes staring over her shoulder and the aroma of cooking spices wafting about. She has since moved up to a real room that's even smaller than my old laundry-room studio—but hers is dominated by a picture window with a commanding view of Pikes Peak.

Ignite Your Creative Passion

Now, with your creative platform firm and secure, the time has arrived to release the passion that is ready to bubble up inside. In other words, it's time to begin your Second Day of Creative Living, when you will learn to ignite your dominant passion and be swept along in its strong, exhilarating flow.

THE SECOND DAY
OF CREATIVE LIVING

The Quest for a
Passionate Heart

Nothing great in the world has been accomplished without passion.

— GEORG WILHELM FRIEDRICH HEGEL

THE FOREST CHAPEL

The Passionate Impulse

Creative passion—the imaginative drive that makes all sorts of discoveries and achievements possible—often seems a mysterious phenomenon. Many people gaze in awe at the intense focus, total absorption, and inspired "flow" of professional painters, writers, or musicians. Then they shake their heads and think, *I could never experience anything like that.*

But in fact, each of us regularly enjoys surges of genuine creative passion, even if only in short bursts. Consider your own life for a moment. Perhaps a moment of such inspiration resulted in a new, more efficient way to achieve a goal at work . . . or provided an unfunded church committee with an unexpected way to help underprivileged kids . . . or opened a door to reconciliation for an estranged relative or acquaintance.

For me, creative passion is the very breath of God, the divine fire within us that gives off sparks of creative excitement, energy, and enthusiasm. Without it, we move mechanically through our daily lives instead of engaging new challenges with every ounce of our being. Some people think creative passion needs to be tamed. I think the inner fire should be fed and exploited, so we can fill the canvas of our lives with the boldest, most exuberant expression possible.

But how might you find and fan the flames of creative passion that lie deep within?

I believe creative passion that has life-changing power usually begins with some extraordinary idea, followed by an irresistible impulse to act on that idea. In other words, you have to be willing every day of your life to follow the little voice within that is nudging you to leap into the unknown and taste life's adventures. Impulses and hunches, which may not seem entirely sensible or even rational at first, are often the spark that ignites the creative fire.

I'm not talking about the kind of impulsiveness that involves blowing $10,000 of your hard-earned money on a fur coat that's on sale, or running off for an illicit weekend with the young hunk at work. Rather, I'm suggesting that we all need to step out boldly to act on the positive inner inclinations and hunches that could jump-start our lives in exciting new directions.

How many times have you felt an impulse to do something, but then held back because you felt too rigid, conventional, or afraid? Maybe the thought crossed your mind to take a day off from your normal routine to go kayaking, but you discounted the idea as frivolous and cleaned out a closet instead. Or perhaps you had a yen to go to a new Bible study or reading group, but opted out because you didn't really know any of the members. Then again, you might have dreamed up an exciting business concept to help people organize their homes or offices, but you just couldn't get off the dime to get started and try it out on somebody.

I believe that such impulses, hunches, and intuitions can be forms of outside guidance, strokes of divine intervention to ignite the spark of passion within. A rigid inner structure—which whispers, "That won't work," or, "Be careful, others will think you're silly"—kills the creative spirit. Giving yourself permission to be a little more spontaneous and intuitive can provide just the needed impetus to break the habits that have dragged you down and start to experience the excitement of living on the creative edge.

I learned this lesson early in my career, with life-changing results. Right after graduating from art school, my friend Jim and I decided to ride the rails coast-to-coast, living an itinerant life as hoboes and sketching along the way. We didn't try to map out all the consequences in advance. We just stepped out on an inner sense that "this is right for us at this particular time in our lives."

My passion for the road set me free—free to go to a far country, well beyond conventional studios, sketchpads, and canvases, where I could dare to test my creativity. While we were riding the rails, Jim and I allowed life itself to do the painting. Unplanned circumstances guided us from day to day, as we took hold of opportunities that came along and followed our impulses. We sketched and daydreamed, and as we sat atop the flatbed cars at night, watching as the stars whizzed by, we came up with a wild idea— an impulsive notion that certainly didn't make such sense for a couple of knockabouts in their early twenties.

"Let's write a book!" we said.

By the time we rolled into New York, we had laid out the entire book in our minds, including the title: *The Artist's Guide to Sketching*. Sure, it was a crazy idea—that twenty-two-year-old artists fresh out of art school could write a book. But what did we have to lose? So we followed our hunch, rented a typewriter, and set up shop in an all-night Burger King on Times Square.

For an entire week, we pounded out the manuscript proposal, living like two homeless people. For the first few nights, we worked during the day and spent the night in a burned-out pier on the Hudson River frequented by tramps and hoboes. But living the hobo life in New York City seemed a little risky, even for a couple of intrepid types like us. After all, people sleeping on benches or in the enclaves of street people in New York City sometimes get into big trouble. So we changed our modus operandi: We wrote at the Burger King at night and slept under park benches with newspapers over our heads by day. What kept us going was our raw passion for the project and a naive optimism that something might just come from the caper.

It was a life I wouldn't want to replicate in today's circumstances, but at the time, the whole plan seemed to make a lot of sense. And as it turned out, we were right to respond to our outrageous impulse. We landed a publisher, earned a small advance, and headed back to California as newly minted authors.

This particular "hobo hunch" catapulted my creative life to new heights. Within weeks of returning to California, Jim and I had parlayed the book into well-paying jobs at Ralph Bakshi Studios, where we fed off each other's talent painting fantasy background art for *Fire and Ice,* an animated adventure film.

My art career was now on its way. Yet if I hadn't acted impulsively to ride the rails with Jim—and continued to go with the creative flow when we came up with the idea to write the book—I suspect I would have lacked the creative force necessary to propel myself to the next level of my career.

So I say, go ahead and follow a whim. Take that spontaneous vacation. Go to an art course to learn watercolor. Spend a morning at the library researching a new subject. Visit that fish camp in the country. Run with an out-of-the-box business concept. Take a cooking class. If you do it once, you'll do it again, and eventually you'll learn to trust your hunches and savor the pleasures of passionate living.

As I've discovered many times in my life, it takes only a single spark to get the fire of passion going. From my experience, passion begets passion. The more you exercise it, the more it grows until you find yourself consumed by the force of its creative power, which can change your life and the lives of others.

But impulse is certainly not the whole story with creative passion. A second, equally important ingredient is an unusual level of optimism—a sense that reaching some seemingly unreachable or impossible goal or ideal is actually possible and within your creative grasp. In other words, you need an outlook on life that I call the "artist's optimistic heart."

The Forest Chapel

GARDEN OF GRACE

The Artist's Optimistic Heart

Creative passion is chronically optimistic.

The most successful creative people I know in most fields—business, health care, nonprofit ventures, science, painting, writing, even politics and religion—are optimistic idealists. They first imagine a superior end product for their creative impulses, and then they plunge into making that abstract image a reality. And they stick with their vision. They incessantly shape, hone, and fine-tune their chosen concept or aspiration because they believe it's actually possible for them to approach an ideal or achieve some sort of perfection.

As for obstacles, they present no major problems to this sanguine mind-set. These creative folks are convinced in their deepest being—in their "heart," if you will—that even the most profound problems at work, at home, or in relationships are fixable. They assume that the most difficult puzzle can be solved and that ultimately, success can be theirs.

How might you develop this kind of optimism? One powerful approach for me has been to find and follow a supremely optimistic model, and early on my youthful imagination discovered a role model in a surprising place: *The Dick Van Dyke Show,* a screwball comedy series from the early days of television. Dick Van Dyke played Rob Petrie, a comedy writer from the suburbs, in this famous 1961–66 CBS hit.

Rob came into my life every week through the tiny black-and-white screen of our family's ancient console TV. Actually, I didn't watch much television as a child because I was always drawing so obsessively. But I never failed to stop what I was doing to catch this particular program so I could study Rob's antics.

To me, Rob's irrepressible, hopeful attitude became an essential component of his creativity. Always looking for a new, fresh way of doing things, he seemed able to come up with brilliant, offbeat concepts out of nowhere. Then, always the optimist and activist, he would immediately try to implement the ideas in his work and life.

The problem was that Rob was a very fallible guy who never tied up all the loose ends. He constantly daydreamed that everything was going to work out perfectly, even though it never quite did. As a result, his impractical nature often got him into trouble.

In one episode, for example, he bought a sailboat, planning to become a skilled sailor. Of course, he almost sank the boat. As I grew older, I recognized Rob's failings as inevitable foibles of the creative person. But these minor faults didn't make him any less compelling. Instead of shrinking away from his character, I continued to find him utterly engaging and worthy of emulation. I knew instinctively that whatever his shortcomings in putting his ideas into practice, the important thing was that he was willing to take a chance to capture his vision of the ideal. And, perhaps most intriguing of all, Rob actually made his living through being creative!

So for me, Rob Petrie embodied the artist's heart—a heart that yearned for goodness, perfection, and light. He lived his life creatively, turning mishaps into moments of laughter and potential disasters into personal triumphs. Episode after episode, I watched enthralled as Rob cheerfully wormed his way out of a mess he had created—such as the time he invited forty-four members of the PTA from his son's school to his TV show, and then forgot they were coming until just before the show went on the air.

Rob represented an irrepressible, buoyant spirit that I wanted to make my own. At some unconscious level, I understood that if I could manage to incorporate Rob Petrie's special qualities into my own personality, I would be much more likely to live my life in a high pitch of creativity. With this hopeful outlook, my ideals would always stay in sight, and with this chronic optimism, I would be motivated to stay on the path to success.

It was only much later, after I realized that the creative life typically is hard and demanding, with rejection lurking around every turn in the road, that I needed a huge dose of idealism and optimism to sustain my forward progress. Otherwise, I might end up a cynic, wallowing in immediate disappointment, anger, bitterness, resentment, and rage. Cynic or idealist—those were the options Rob Petrie presented, and it was obvious that the choice was up to me.

Perhaps now you can understand a little better why I believe that to achieve *your* highest creative goals, a vast reservoir of optimism must accompany every effective artistic impulse. We need to develop a vision of where we want to go or what we want to be, and then become convinced we can actually capture an ideal that has the power to dominate the imagination.

If you have this artist's optimistic heart, something inside will always compel you to take an additional step to make things just a little better—to shape that lump of clay into a beautiful vase, to weld pieces of assembled junk into a majestic piece of sculpture, to put an extra touch or two on that business report, or to go the second mile in that relationship.

From an early age, I began to create in my mind the image of the kind of man I wanted to be and the kind of life I would lead as an artist and as a person. Even as a child, I began to aspire to live out my entire life as though it were a work of art. And the artist's heart of enthusiasm and passion for life still beats within me to this day. I see life as a series of choices that can either rob me of my idealism and optimism, or empower me with lasting passion and expectation.

PERSEVERANCE

The Power to Overcome

A characteristic feature of true creative passion is that it contains the power to consistently overcome hardship and rejection. Unlike most fleeting enthusiasms, creative passion pushes through and prevails—ignoring even the most committed naysayers and surmounting apparently insuperable obstacles.

Of course, it's not easy to confront rejection and criticism day after day, or project after project, without becoming discouraged or immobilized. Yet without the grit that overcomes practically any difficulty, passion will surely wilt, and failure will quickly overwhelm the potential for success. As you begin to feel the stirrings of creative passion deep in your soul, the main challenge is to find some way to transform those temporary surges of creativity into a sustained, potent stream that will overwhelm every doubt, frustration, and seemingly impenetrable barrier.

Yet for most of us, this kind of strong, sustained imaginative passion doesn't materialize out of thin air. Almost everyone who seeks to unleash true creative passion must embark on a reconsideration of his or her personal worldview or basic philosophy of life. The passion that prevails over rejection and hardship must be, above all, a passion that emanates from a profound personal belief system.

In my own case, I've noticed that irresistible passion bursts forth only when I consciously accept the fact that God is actually in control of my life and daily circumstances. In other words, creative passion intensifies as I become acutely aware that things don't just happen to me randomly. When the unexpected occurs, I know beyond any doubt that every challenge I confront is there for a purpose. To put this another way, I believe every environment I encounter has been divinely planned to maximize my personal creativity and growth.

From a creative viewpoint, this means that there are really no coincidences in our lives. Regardless of your particular circumstances, God has placed you in exactly the right position to jump-start and hone your imagination and productivity. Sometimes even the most difficult environment may serve as an impetus for the most significant surge of creativity.

If I ever doubt this observation—if I think it's too naively optimistic for the real world—I reflect for a moment on the circumstances of my own early years. I suppose it would have been easy for me to give up before I got started if I had dwelt on the limitations of my environment: a broken home, the absence of a strong male role model, a tiny shared room in a small, run-down house, and no resources for years to buy the materials necessary to learn and practice the craft of painting.

Yet I know that step-by-step throughout my childhood, divine Providence plopped me down in modest, often stressful environments because the circumstances somehow contained the power to cause me to grow, toughen, and learn—and maximize my creative potential. Most of the time, it was only much later that I realized the importance of certain extremely significant but not-so-coincidental events. For example, during my early teen years, a well-regarded artist and university professor of art named Glen Wessels built his retirement studio across the field from my family's cramped rural home. Eventually, I had the opportunity to work for him and learn some secrets of painting and the creative life that might never have been communicated to me if I had grown up in another, more affluent neighborhood.

The intervention of such divinely ordained surprises has been more the rule than the exception in my life. Unplanned events and encounters—which enrich my life immeasurably—seem to occur at least as often as those things I expect or schedule. Many times, the circumstances begin as a negative—a situation or experience I would rather avoid entirely. But if I'm patient and watchful, more often than not the negative morphs into the positive, and the uncreative into the creative. That's what happened to my good friend Josh McDowell, the renowned Christian thinker and apologist.

Over lunch one day, Josh explained to me that his father had been the town drunk. The McDowells had lived on a farm, and more often than not, Josh would come home from school to find his mother beaten and lying in the gutter, because his father was drunk again.

"Why did God pick me for such a family?" Josh asked rhetorically. "Why would I, as a little kid, have to suffer the pain of going to the barbershop, where the barber would take one look at me and say, 'Oh, you're Joe McDowell's son—that drunk.'"

The pain, the stabbing verbal wounds, the embarrassment—I could identify with all of it. As Josh talked, I thought of my own dad, who was an embittered World War II veteran. The rumors of his womanizing, the memories of his fights with my mom, the snide remarks from my friends about their divorce, and the disappointment I felt at his not being around can still sting if I dwell on them.

"Why me?" Josh asked again. The reason, he said, was simple: "If I had had the dad I wanted, I wouldn't have become the Josh McDowell I have become. I would have been someone else."

For Josh, a large part of God's plan was to prepare and sharpen him to handle hard questions and challenges, especially those posed by young people searching for the meaning of life. Because he had been through the toughest of personal circumstances, he had learned how to respond powerfully to a barrage of verbal abuse and mockery. So he was emotionally and spiritually well-prepared—and difficult to rattle—when he finally embarked on his life's work with college students who asked hard questions about the ultimate purpose of life. His early life-lessons gave him the ability to respond creatively and spontaneously to the challenges he later confronted during debates.

God has a plan for you, too, and once you understand that plan, you'll be in a position to formulate a positive vision of what your life—and your creative goals—should be. Your creative vision can be as big as your imagination and as far-reaching as anything you can dream. Just as important, the power of such a God-rooted creativity will enable you to overcome and prevail as you meet the inevitable rejections that will threaten you with discouragement.

So regardless of how confining or hostile your present circumstances may seem, in reality you are free—free to grab hold of life with all the creativity and joyfulness that God can bestow. Or as the psalmist said, "In thy presence there is fulness of joy" (Ps. 16:11 RSV).

I understood those truths, even as a child, even before I could cite the Bible, chapter and verse. And so I grabbed hold of the dream, laid it out in my mind, layered it, colored it, painted it broadly, and then added the fine details, those "payoff details" that make a painting spring to life. In that dream, I was not only an artist who could push through fear, a lack of confidence, and rejection as I filled a blank sheet of paper with radiant images; I was also an effective father, husband, employee, friend, and business owner—a man who had the power to prevail over the ordinary problems and difficulties of life.

Under sufficient pressure, a lump of coal becomes a diamond. Similarly, under the harshest circumstances—the worst environments imaginable, which seem to make creativity totally impossible—your discomfort should serve as a reminder that you are slowly being prepared for great things. So don't allow anger, frustration, or fear to interfere with the shaping process. Every environment you experience is really a divinely ordained kiln that is poised to produce great creativity.

Perseverance

BRIDGE OF HOPE

Finding Your Focus

reative passion is focused passion.

It's an inner drive that stays on message, with ultimate objectives and goals always in clear view. Conversely, perhaps the greatest enemy of productive, sustained creativity is the seductive, often well-meaning impulse that diverts us from the important task at hand. So many times, interrupting the creative flow may seem justified, such as when we get a phone call from a relative who wants to chat . . . a last-minute opportunity to go to brunch with a close friend . . . or an e-mail that begs for a long, thoughtful response. But if we spontaneously stop work and respond to such interruptions—instead of scheduling a response for a later time—we risk losing focus.

Let's face it: Many of us have multiple interests, and we may even muse about how great it would be to change into three or four people instead of being one. Think of how much more you could accomplish if you were four people! But of course, that's a pipe dream. I'm only one person, with a limited amount of time to work each day, and the same holds true for you.

So even though intense, creative work tends to intensify our interest in many intellectual, spiritual, and artistic areas, these blasts of inspiration may also operate as a double-edged sword. In effect, an overactive imagination can actually begin to work against your ability to refine and finish existing projects. In short, it's all too easy to become overly excited about the "creative flavor of the moment."

You may get sidetracked from your most important creative passion for any number of good reasons. For example, you might turn away from your important task at hand when a friend suggests an intriguing idea for a new moneymaking scheme, or when some outrageous news report tempts you to draft a letter to the editor, or when a worthy but time-consuming request comes in to work on a charitable fund drive.

Certainly, many such ideas may have some merit. But on balance, they become negative influences in your life when they cause your thought and work patterns to become scattered. In fact, the only way most people can maximize their creative abilities and produce something significant is to pare down the creative possibilities. So your ultimate goal must be to achieve a single laser-focus on the one project that really matters most of all.

Because my primary creative focus in life has always been my art, I constantly try to keep my eyes riveted at all times on more effective ways to draw and paint. Specifically, I try to avoid all distractions that might get in the way of my effort to depict the light-permeated reality in nature that I believe reflects the reality of God's presence among us.

But I'm certainly not perfect. Sometimes, despite all my efforts and convictions to the contrary, I temporarily lose my focus. Outside pressures or concerns at times invade my studio and interfere with my primary creative impulse. I get distracted or sidetracked from my painting because, in the overly active mind that characterizes most people who are on a "creative roll," I begin to speculate and embroider some new business concept or replay ways to improve or restore a particular personal relationship. In such situations, I have to take a step back from the easel, breathe deeply a couple of times, and find a way to return to my primary creative focus.

One helpful approach might be to fill your mind with a line from some great thinker that encourages single-minded focus. You might pick an appropriate line from Shakespeare, such as the phrase "one thing constant" from Balthasar's song in *Much Ado About Nothing* (act 2, scene 3).

As I turn such words over and over in my mind, I find my tumultuous thoughts settling down. Then, I can return with a single focus to the task at hand. Or I might choose a favorite Bible verse that suggests clear focus and indomitable effort, such as "The LORD is one" (Deut. 6:4 NKJV), "I can do all things through Christ" (Phil. 4:13 NKJV), or "My eyes are ever toward the LORD" (Ps. 25:15 RSV). After contemplating such passages for several minutes, the distracting "noise" in my mind dissipates, extraneous thoughts begin to recede, and my ability to focus confidently on my work returns.

On other occasions, with nothing more than a simple act of the will, I may be able to shift my conscious thoughts back to the task at hand—usually, the painting that is sitting in front of me on my easel. After I concentrate on the lines and colors for a few moments, my original vision of the painting will usually fill my mind again—and I find I'm back on my creative track.

Others have achieved remarkable focus on their creative work by manipulating their physical environment. I'm reminded, for instance, of the writer Stephen King, who distinguishes between "receiving" and "transmitting" places when he is seeking laser-sharp attention in his creative work.

Most of King's *receiving* of creative inspiration occurs when he is reading—and that means selecting a comfortable spot where the lighting is good, outside influences are shut out, and "the vibe is usually strong," he says in *On Writing* (2000, 104). For him, this receiving location is a particular blue chair in his study.

King's *transmitting* phase for creativity is his writing space, where he typically turns out a minimum of ten pages, or two thousand words, per day. According to King, he settled on his basement, where he placed a handmade desk, his blue reading chair, and other accoutrements. He recommends no phones, TV, video games, or other distractions. Also, he says, "if there's a window, draw the curtains or pull down the shades . . . your writing room should be private, a place where you go to dream" (156–57).

As you know, I have a somewhat different approach to my own creative space. But when it comes to striving for a high degree of concentration, I can certainly identify with many of King's principles—such as achieving maximum privacy and avoiding all unnecessary distractions.

On a very personal level, I was particularly impressed with his revelation about his early makeshift study where he wrote his first two novels, *Carrie* and *Salem's Lot*: He achieved privacy—and focus—by working in the converted laundry room of a trailer on a portable Olivetti typewriter at a child's desk. Sound familiar?

But perhaps the most dramatic illustration of creative focus I've encountered involved the late western novelist Louis L'Amour. On at least one occasion, as a stunt, L'Amour set up a typewriter on the divider of a major highway, with cars whizzing by from either direction. Then he would proceed to bang out a chapter of one of his books.

How could he perform such a feat, which required incredible concentration, not to mention a degree of fearlessness, in the face of oncoming traffic?

I have to attribute much of L'Amour's mental toughness and focus as a mature writer to the unstable, rough-and-tumble physical challenges that distinguished his early life as a cowboy and professional boxer. Many times, it seems, he really didn't have a "creative place" that he could call his own—certainly no fixed studio, special writing room, or other creativity-nurturing environment, at least not in the conventional sense of the term.

But despite the challenging physical circumstances, he always seemed able to find a stable center inside himself, which positioned him to do his best work. His remarkable ability to focus in any situation enabled him to filter out distractions; even amid near-total outside chaos, he still could write coherent, compelling stories.

The result was that L'Amour succeeded beyond most writers' wildest dreams. Because of his disciplined focus on his artistic priorities, he was able to be highly efficient in evaluating the details, facts, and other raw material that would be most useful later when he sat down to write a story. The fast-drawing, straight-shooting marksmen and hardfisted wranglers he had encountered in the tight spaces and hard knocks of his youth eventually ended up between the covers of his popular novels, such as *Mojave Crossing, Shalako,* and *The Sackett Brand.* Your goal should also be to define and then maintain your creative focus, no matter how chaotic the outside pressures and circumstances.

For most people, the very first step in achieving superior creative focus should be just to assume that you will inevitably—and probably frequently—confront serious threats to your concentration. Everyone who aspires to great creativity must at one time or another respond to the crying child, the needy spouse, the demanding boss, or some other external pressure of daily life. These disruptive forces are part of the human condition, and our human duty to others often *demands* that we respond.

But in the end, the prize of significant achievement will go to those who can rise above distractions—and enter a tranquil realm of the mind and spirit where creativity reigns. The challenge, then, is to learn to harness and direct your creative passion in any and all circumstances. Passion without purpose may become destructive, but properly focused passion can become a powerful force for boundless creativity.

STAIRWAY TO PARADISE

Called to Create

Creative passion is a way of life.

In other words, to have a life-changing impact, fleeting inspiration must be translated into a true *calling*—or a daily commitment to implement the creative impulse. When we are called to some great task or goal in life, we wake up in the morning thinking about it. And we feel anxious or guilty if we haven't devoted sufficient hours during a given day to the creative goal.

Because I'm totally committed as an artist, I have always tended to place the highest importance on spending long, high-quality hours on my work. Also, if I have some free time, my mind will inevitably wander back to some unfinished painting sitting in my studio, and as new ideas rush into my mind, I'll start itching to get back in front of my easel. Or if I become distracted or sidetracked by other concerns of daily life, I won't feel quite right until the brush is once again in my hand.

This sort of built-in passion makes it relatively easy for me to plunge enthusiastically into my creative efforts practically every day of my life. But what is it that convinces me I am truly called to the work that I do— to the endeavors to which I devote most of my waking hours?

For many who are in search of a true calling, the first place to look may be an early and ongoing passion, often accompanied by some natural skill. This natural passion may continue to attract us, no matter how old we get or what other demands of life intervene.

From what I've pieced together about my early years, I've decided that I must have been born with a passion to create works of art. I could actually draw before I could walk. The way my mother tells the story, I was on the floor crawling around in my corduroy overalls, when she handed me a crayon. With my chubby little left hand, I reached out, grabbed the colorful stick of wax, and held it tight, as though I had received the most precious gift in the world.

From that moment on, every time I had a crayon in my hand, I felt an abiding sense of comfort. It was better than a bottle, better even than a hug. The crayon served as a key to a warm, light-filled inner home—a place of profound security that tapped into who I really was and what I was created to be.

By the time I was five, drawing had become second nature, and I now know I had a natural talent because I could see with eyes beyond my years and range of experience. I can remember vividly coming upon my sister, Katey, who is seven years older than me, as she worked on a drawing of a house near some railroad tracks. Next to the house, she had sketched in the tracks, representing them as two parallel lines. The minute I saw the tracks, I knew what was wrong.

"It goes this way," I said, grabbing her pencil to rework her drawing.

As carefully as I could, I drew the two lines converging on the horizon in what I now know is called linear perspective. For a trained artist, drawing in perspective isn't terribly sophisticated, but for a five-year-old, the illusion of a third-dimensional depth on a two-dimensional sheet of paper seemed an astonishing discovery.

Bursting with pride, I stared at the drawing in wonderment. The picture looked real and three-dimensional, all because of the way I had drawn the lines on the paper. I couldn't believe it was possible to take a flat piece of paper and create the illusion of a special world, and yet, there it was. Out of nowhere I had unearthed a significant insight that came from a visual memory of reality somewhere deep within. I can't explain why I knew what to draw—I just knew. In that moment of recognition, something ignited inside me, and I could feel myself gripped by an urgency to create. As simple as my drawing was, it pushed my creative buttons profoundly, propelling me yet another step forward toward my calling.

But on reflection, I realize it wasn't attention or approval that inspired me in those early days, though I have to admit I enjoyed the accolades.

What inspired me most was my own delight in seeing that my creative powers were improving. I like to think my response must have been similar to the delight God felt when he created the universe and said, "It is good."

Most likely, your situation is somewhat different from mine. Unlike me, you may not be able to point to just one great passion that has gripped you since you were a small child. Or perhaps you have *several* strong interests, and you have trouble deciding which should be given priority. Then again, if you're like many people, you may find that you really can't put your finger on any candidates for a dominant creative passion in your life, much less how you might express such a passion in your daily life.

But even though you may not sense such a strong, long-standing creative drive to express yourself in a particular way, it certainly doesn't mean you don't have your own special calling. I've become convinced that *everyone* has an innate urge to create something, even if at first that urge remains hidden.

Finding your particular calling may take a little time and effort, but the process really isn't very complicated. To make things as easy as possible, I have decided to end this Second Day of Creative Living with an action plan that you may find helpful as you search for your own calling.

MAKE A WISH COTTAGE

Igniting Your Passion

Perhaps the best way to begin your quest for your great, passionate calling in life is simply to ask yourself this question: "If I could spend my time doing one thing for one week, what would that one thing be?"

As you reflect on this query, you may come up with something as simple as reading your child a fanciful story at bedtime. Or your response may be as challenging as working on an intellectual skill, such as starting that novel you've been yearning to write, or learning a new language so that you can broaden your contact with other cultures.

Maybe you would devote that creative week to reading the entire Bible through for the first time in your life. Or maybe you feel a need to restore some old friendships, a process that may involve delving deep within yourself to forgive someone who has hurt you.

The one-week project you have chosen most likely has something to do with your calling, as well as with your primary passion in life. In fact, more often than not, the two are one and the same. Now, to continue with this exercise—and to identify your calling and your dominant creative passion more precisely—try this sequence of creative acts:

Retire to a Quiet Setting—a Favorite Room, Wooded Walk, or Vista

Now is the time to head for the special creative place that you prepared a few pages back on your "First Day of Creative Living." Be sure to take your journal or a writing notebook with you.

I keep a notebook in my pocket wherever I go, to capture spontaneous insights. It's with me at church, at my ranch, and even in business meetings. On its pages, I record joyous moments of serendipity: a chance conversation with an old friend, a concept for a new painting, a playful interlude with one of my kids, an unusual marketing idea for my business.

Spend at Least an Hour in Prayer, Meditation, or Quiet Thought

As you sit quietly, focus on this question, which is a broader version of the one-week exercise that began this chapter: "What is the single most important thing I should do with the rest of my life?"

I ask myself this question daily. Even though I have understood my "single most important thing" since childhood, I never fail to revisit the question in order to evaluate where I stand in relation to my goals at any given moment. Focusing on your own "most important thing" will not only help you fine-tune your understanding of what it is, the exercise will also help you establish priorities in making your ideal a reality.

Jot Down Your Random Thoughts and Insights

I've found it absolutely essential to record regularly what I'm thinking so that I can build a reliable record of my ideas and thought processes. No matter how smart you are or how good you think your memory is, you're sure to forget flashes of insight as time goes by.

But as you write, keep this principle in mind: Candidates for your "single most important thing" do not have to be career choices or money-making propositions, although they could be. For many people, their most significant lifework goes unpaid. For me, my life's work and my art go hand in hand. Yet, paid or unpaid, I would keep doing it.

Imagine Ways You Can Change Lives

As you free-associate about your dominant passion and calling, remember that there's nothing like serving others to stimulate the kind of creativity that is lasting. The act can be as simple as leading singing once a week in a nursing home or as grandiose as organizing a mission project to refugee camps in Africa. Sometimes, all it takes to make a difference in someone's life is a little conversation.

A few years ago, I was jogging around town exploring some of the old neighborhoods, when I stumbled onto a little cardboard shack. It looked just like the makeshift shelters I had seen along the rail lines during my months as an itinerant artist. Ever since those days, I've been fascinated by street people and befriend them whenever I can.

This time was no different. Without a moment's hesitation, I jogged up to the shack and knocked on the door. A few seconds later, the door opened to reveal a shaggy old guy who introduced himself as "Vic." He invited me in and introduced me to his dogs, and for an hour or so we sat on ramshackle chairs chatting about life. We've been friends ever since.

Ultimately, though, our conversations spawned more than a friendship. In part due to my encouragement, Vic took up painting, and when the local soup kitchen held an art show, some of his work went up for sale.

"This could be a handle for you to get your life stable again," I told him.

Vic exhibited his paintings and sold a few—more than one to a fellow artist named Kinkade. Now, he's living in a little rental room in a house with heat and running water. Whenever I see him with a painting in his hand, chances are I'll dip into my pocket and add it to my collection. Those paintings serve as a reminder of why I do what I do—and an assurance that my own light is not shining in vain.

Choose Two or Three Insights That Seem Most Significant

In only one session of contemplation, most people can't immediately settle on just one overriding passion for their lives. After all, this is an extremely important decision you're trying to make—and important decisions often take much time and reflection.

So at this point, feel free to include several possibilities for your calling and great creative passion. Life and time will have a way of refining your list.

Sleep on Your Insights

I try never to plunge into a major decision without allowing at least one full day and night for my ideas to ripen. Many times, what seems a great idea will emerge as a not-so-good idea after a night's sleep.

⟶ *Return to Your Quiet Place—and Project Your Passions onto a Big Screen*

If you think you've found the "finalists" for your calling, try to imagine what each passionate impulse would look like when carried to an extreme. You might picture your vision in the hands of a producer like Steven Spielberg or Cecil B. DeMille. Or you could think of the most outlandish, bizarre possibilities by asking yourself, "What if?"

⟶ "*What if* I took my business to a national level?"
⟶ "*What if* my wife and I left the kids with Grandma and went hiking in the Rockies?"
⟶ "*What if* I learned to speak Chinese?"

I asked myself such questions as a young artist with startling results. After my stint at the movie studio, I began to have some success selling my paintings in galleries. I was churning out western landscapes, rural subjects, and ranch scenes, and they were flying out of the galleries at a hundred dollars each. One went to a Chinese businessman who bought the painting for his office in Hong Kong. Another found its way into the hands of a young couple from Colorado, who planned to make it the centerpiece of their formal living room.

My paintings were being snapped up, and I was paying my bills. But I was frustrated. I realized that if I continued on the current track, I could plug away like this for the rest of my life, only to have the few people who could afford original paintings have a chance to see my work.

"*What if* I found a way to take my paintings to a wider audience?" I asked myself. "*What if* I could replicate the paintings? *What if* people all over the world could see the art I create?"

A grandiose vision, you say? The folly of an inveterate dreamer?

Not at all. The what-ifs began to turn into reality a couple of years later when I happened upon a print with brushwork so real it looked like an original oil painting. I tracked down the artist and then the printer, and using our life savings of $5,000, my wife and I created our first limited-edition print. Our business, and the chance to share my paintings with people the world over, grew from that tiny seed. So why not ask, "What if?"

∽ *Choose One Dominant, Authentic Passion*

After you complete the "What if" exercise, the chances are that one interest will rise above all others as the dominant passion in your life. That's the one you want to cultivate with your available energy and time. But before you move ahead, I'd suggest a crucial test—the test of authenticity.

At heart, a truly authentic passion is one you are willing to pursue privately, even if there's no money to be made or fame to be acquired. You probably won't believe this until you're in a position to experience it, but I've learned over the years that no audience applause or rave review is ultimately fulfilling. The only success that means anything is victory in the inner creative battle, the conflict that rages as you struggle toward the goals you have set for yourself.

For me, the main affirmation of my drawing and painting has always come from within. For years I didn't have any place to sell my drawings or a gallery to show them. The greatest fulfillment I got as a child—and still get now—is a private fulfillment.

This is fortunate because I'm alone every day. I don't associate with many people during my working hours, and I don't show my in-progress paintings to anyone except my wife, Nanette. Usually, I finish a painting and never see anyone's reaction to it. I hand it to my assistant, and she has it transported to my publishing company to begin the printmaking process. Sometimes, the management of the company will stage a big unveiling of the new piece, but often I'm not present. Furthermore, I don't need to be there for my creative affirmation. All I need now is the same thing I needed at age five: the inner knowledge that I had achieved what I set out to do.

So now, you've done all you can by yourself to identify the great passion of your life. But I always advise those seeking a major creative outlet to look beyond themselves to the wisdom of others.

∽ *Test Your Final Choice on Trusted Advisers and Soul Mates*

Ask your advisers a question like this: "Could you see me devoting a significant part of my time and energy to [*your calling or great passion*]?"

If you get a unanimous "yes" to such a question, that will give you some idea that perhaps you're not on a creative wild-goose chase. Of course, sometimes, the most creative people listen to only their personal inner muse—and ignore what anyone else says. Occasionally, it turns out that they are right and everyone else is wrong. But more often, seeking outside advice is the wiser course of action before making a major commitment of time or money to some project.

I always bounce every new idea—whether an inspiration for a painting or for a new business deal—off my wife, Nanette, who for years has served as my personal counterbalance, the one I trust most with my dreams and aspirations. I know that, above all, she has my best interests at heart, and she will always be sensitive to the bigger picture for us and for our family.

After you've tested your chosen passion and creative calling with others, you're ready to see how well your choice works in the real world. In other words, the time has arrived to act.

Act on Your Passion

Two women I know got together over lunch to share their passions. One was a writer who had a passion for helping kids; the other was a real-estate agent who felt a burning desire to expand the cultural vision of her community in Vero Beach, Florida. Together, they came up with an idea to create a series of writing workshops for teenagers. Their idea was simple: introduce teens to professional writers at free half-day workshops, which would be underwritten by grants and private donations.

Six months later, they launched the first workshop with twenty teenagers and a novelist known for his political thrillers. Spurred by their passion, the Teen Writers Workshop mushroomed over the next three years, ultimately reaching hundreds of students.

But the women didn't stop there. They took the program into a local prison for teenage felons, to provide the young men a way through their writing to "break out" creatively. Now the women have gone global, by introducing the Teen Writers Workshop in Vietnam. Yet this workshop vision started rather modestly, through a collaboration involving two friends with a mutual passion for something bigger than themselves, and the cheerleading spirit to make it happen.

These are just a few suggestions to help you find, channel, and fan the flames of your great passion in life—the inner creative drive that can serve as a great source of personal realization and satisfaction. Now, let's move on to the Third Day of Creative Living—a day that will focus on the marvelous experience of true love.

THE THIRD DAY
OF CREATIVE LIVING

The Experience of True Love

Faith, hope, love abide, these three; but the greatest of these is love.

— APOSTLE PAUL, 1 CORINTHIANS 13:13 RSV

SWEETHEART COTTAGE II

A Stairway of Love

Whenever we hear the word *love* these days, there's an initial tendency to think of a sexual relationship. The phrase "making love" always seems to carry that connotation— and that's the message we typically hear and see on TV, in the movies, and in popular literature.

As a red-blooded American male, I certainly celebrate the joy of the sexual union. After all, God created it for our benefit. But I do think it's unfortunate that in limiting love to the bedroom, our culture has lost the broader, richer meaning of the term that the ancient Scriptures wrapped up in the Greek word *agape*.

This profound concept, agape, which is translated "love" in the Apostle Paul's "Love Chapter" in the Bible (1 Corinthians 13) and elsewhere, encompasses so much more than physical expressions of affection or passion. Often described as the noblest, purest, and most powerful kind of love, agape emanates from the very heart of God. And I believe this supernatural force is the very soul of *true* love in our human and divine relationships.

Just as important, true agape love is an essential ingredient as we strive for creativity in our work, avocations, and relationships. A painting without love will often become a flat, passionless, even destructive expression of the worst side of human nature. Long ago, I resolved that I would always work to create imagery that affirmed life-positive values and celebrated the beauty and subtlety of nature. I concluded that if I depicted the destructive or negative aspects of human experience, I would contribute to cultural deterioration and the general hopelessness that often permeates the modern outlook. But if I could somehow find a spark of light and truth in my subjects—and project that spark onto the canvas—my creative passion might be transformed into a force for good, rather than for darkness.

In considering how agape love might enter my creative work as a painter, I have found it helpful to meditate regularly, in a kind of stair-step fashion, on how love resides on multiple levels in my life. Of course, it all starts with the power of God's love: "For God so loved the world . . . ," including me. After God's Spirit embraces me in a meaningful way, I am able to express his love on so many other levels:

— First, love of my wife.
— Then, love of my children.
— Next, love of my parents.
— Next, love of brothers, sisters, and friends.
— Finally, love of my work and for those with whom I
  share it.

As I reflect on how true love plays out on each of these planes of existence, I learn more and more about what the highest form of love really means. It's as though I'm mounting a kind of ladder to heaven, and the higher I go, the more I see and learn. My understanding of my wife informs my insights into my children. My devotion to my children, in turn, provides a platform for me to understand more fully my interactions with friends. Finally, the totality of all these love relationships elevates me into a new involvement with my work. My painting is nothing more than a culminating expression of my relationships with others and with God.

Perhaps this notion of a "creative stairway of love" could be helpful to you as well. To try it out, picture the potential love relationships in your life: spouse, children, friends, or outsiders you want to touch with your creative passion—and also, God.

Of course, you may be missing some of these relationships. For example, perhaps you're not married or you don't have children or you're an only child. That's perfectly all right because at certain junctures of life, all of us find we're missing common relationships. Yet a profound experience of love is still possible.

Remember this fundamental truth: *All* of us at *all* times possess the potential to love and be loved. Friends—or potential friends—are always there. Your creative passion, your calling, is always there. And certainly, God is always there. It's just a matter of reaching out and exploring the relationships in your life until you reach the level of love you are meant to enjoy. So join me now as we climb the stairway of love.

SWEETHEART COTTAGE

The Servant Spouse

For those of us who are married, the most profound creative encounter with love begins with our spouses. If profound agape love permeates that relationship, each partner will secure a potent platform to pursue creative endeavors in other areas of life.

But if true love is absent from a marriage, each spouse is likely to become entangled in dissatisfactions, unmet expectations, frustration, or anger. Eventually, the result may be a deeply troubled or broken relationship that saps emotional and spiritual energies, and makes maximum creativity impossible in other avenues of life.

So how do we find the marital love that will provide fertile soil for broader creativity? It's been said that love is best defined not by what it is, but by what it does. That's really the main message of 1 Corinthians 13, where agape love is described as "patient and kind." This kind of love "bears all things, believes all things, hopes all things, endures all things."

Similarly, the ultimate test of true love in marriage is how well we treat—and serve—that husband or wife. Yes, I did say "serve," because I don't think the real potential for love comes into focus for the married among us until we learn to assume a sacrificial stance toward our spouse.

I realize these are provocative words for some people, given the cultural battles on religion, marriage, and morality now raging in American society. But hear me out. I'm *not* saying that the wife or husband should blindly be at the beck and call of a spouse's whims, reasonable or not. Rather, the only way that real love can permeate and control a marital relationship—and open the door to greater creativity in every dimension of life—is for *both parties in the relationship to give with no expectation of return.*

A marriage can never become the power source for maximum creativity in life if each person operates on the assumption that "I'll contribute my fifty percent to this deal, and no more." Rather, each person must be prepared to give all—and even more—to the other, if need be.

If you think about it, this approach is only logical and reasonable. For example, you might assume that as a professional painter, with a wife who is not a professional painter, I just operate completely independently of her. In other words, you might believe I exist in a kind of professional bubble that she never enters.

Yet nothing could be farther from the truth. Throughout the day, Nanette enters my creative world by managing minor details of supplies, maintenance, and errands; fending off visitors and interruptions; and working with my assistant to manage my ongoing schedule. She's always available for a quick critique of the painting I'm working on, and when I need a sounding board for a new idea, she's never too busy to talk, often by the hour, until we both attain new insights. At the end of the day, when I need friendship or just simple encouragement, she acts as my trusted friend, as we sit together in our reading chairs and share a few quiet moments.

I know it's not easy for Nanette to give me these segments of her precious time, but she responds willingly and generously—because she knows that we are a true partnership, a team with two wholly committed members. Furthermore, from Nanette's perspective, the list of ways I support and encourage her throughout each day would be similarly extensive. The work and well-being of one coincide perfectly with the work and well-being of the other. And when one slips into the fallacy of believing "I've got to draw a line here or there," both will suffer.

Reflect for a moment on your past relationship with your spouse. At different times, one of you has undoubtedly been more vulnerable or needy than the other. At such times, one or the other of you has desperately needed emotional or financial support, deep personal encouragement, or even physical aid. A spouse with a fifty-fifty mentality would never be able to respond lovingly and effectively to that kind of hurt or want.

Long before I was married, I came to understand that sometimes, my future wife would need all my time, energy, and attention—and other times, I would require the same level of support from her. In many ways, I think, my experience of coming from a broken family made me more sensitive to the need to go the extra mile with a spouse—that is, if I really want to make the relationship work.

How might you bring this sacrificial servant-spouse dynamic into your own marriage? Whenever anger, frustration, or misunderstanding intrudes into your relationship—and threatens to poison the creative impulses elsewhere in your life—I'd suggest this simple exercise:

First, avoid at all costs the temptation to point the finger of blame at your spouse. Don't nag, lecture, or reprimand, even if it's absolutely clear to you that you are right and your husband or wife is wrong. Instead, ask yourself, "What can *I* do to set things right?"

That's a rather creative question—or more accurately, it's a question that calls for creative decision-making and action. It works against any tendency to attach blame. Instead, as you shine the spotlight on yourself, you automatically recognize that you have the power or wherewithal to take the initiative and get the relationship back on track again.

When I apply this principle in my own marriage, I am often reminded of my experience as a painter. If I decide that one of my sketches, or my choice of composition, or my selection of colors isn't quite right, I don't blame my canvas, paintbrushes, or anybody or anything else. Instead, I look in the mirror and pose the same question I ask of my marriage relationship: "What can *I* do to set things right?"

Just the willingness to ask the question is usually enough to reorient my thinking and turn things around—both in painting and more important, in my relationship with Nanette. But maintaining a servant's heart attitude is just the first step in achieving a creative, loving relationship. Next, you have to use your imagination to paint a more detailed mental picture of what a perfect marriage should look like.

SEASIDE HIDEAWAY

Vision of a Perfect Marriage

To accomplish anything creatively, you must first have a vision. From somewhere, a flash of insight—an ideal picture of where you ultimately want to go—must fill your mind and imagination. Then, with that vivid image in mind, the creative process proceeds with an overriding purpose and flow that takes on a life of its own.

This creative vision can appear in an instant when you're exposed to some highly stimulating environment or other outside influence, or it may emerge gradually, after months or years of struggle. In the artistic arena, the life-changing inspiration may seem to materialize instantaneously, out of nowhere. The same may be true of a paradigm-shaking idea you come up with at work.

But in relationships, the transforming vision often takes more time and may develop piecemeal in assuming its final form and richness. That's especially true of a marriage relationship, which, as we learn over the years, can be so much more complex and profound than most of us ever anticipated when we were caught up in the heady romance of courtship.

In some ways, I had a head start in formulating my own vision for a creative marriage. As a youngster, I observed firsthand that if a husband or wife focuses primarily on individual needs and interests, the relationship will immediately be in jeopardy. But the precise details, the exact colors and shapes of my vision of marriage, didn't begin to emerge until I was a thirteen-year-old with a paper route—and Nanette's family became my customers.

From the moment we met as young teenagers, Nanette was part of my broad creative vision, part of the scenario I wanted to create for my entire life. Of course, I was in many ways an immature adolescent when I first became enamored of her. But even while we were still in grade school, I pictured us married, sharing our deepest aspirations from sunup to sunset, having kids, working side by side. And I saw us growing old together, holding hands, laughing and joking and remembering. It was as though I had been provided at a very young age with an inner paintbrush that enabled me in my imagination to create a detailed painting of an ideal marriage.

You may wonder how a kid from a broken home could have conjured up such an idealized vision of a long-range marriage. For whatever reason, as long as I can remember, instead of being hostile to marriage for fear of replicating my parents' experience, I have embraced the idea of a marriage relationship wholeheartedly.

On the deepest level, I believe those positive visions have been part of my total creative calling in life. As a preteen, I regularly envisioned the husband-wife relationship afresh through the romantic eye of a budding artist. Just as I now take pains to choose the right colors for my palette, I began preselecting the images that one day would enliven the canvas of my marriage. In my youthful mind, with Nanette always the center of the vision, I pictured the perfect life partner and the perfect relationship. And day by day, I added insights about what this ideal marriage would look like.

Perhaps the very first such insight came from my mother. Despite her two failed marriages and a history of divorce that seemed to plague the family like a curse, she spoke about marriage reverentially.

The way my mother envisioned it, marriage was meant to be the deepest experience imaginable for a human being, the heaven-on-earth that God intends for a man and a woman together. It was a gift, a blessing, a union of two bodies and souls that could elevate life beyond its mundane duties and experiences into something precious, sacramental.

Mom's view of marriage was so pure, and her belief in its meaning so palpable, that I couldn't help but fall captive to the vision. From my earliest memory I wanted such a relationship, but I knew that to achieve it, I would need more than just wishful thinking.

"With God all things are possible," my mom exhorted, and I believed her. I knew down deep that if I found the perfect partner and put God at the center of our relationship, I could indeed open the door to a soul-satisfying life partnership.

My mom exerted a significant early impact on my vision, but she wasn't the only influence.

As the vision unfolded, it was my neighbor and artistic mentor, Glen Wessels, who taught me that the ideal marriage outlined by my mother marked only the beginning of a satisfying relationship. More than an idealized romance or even a sweet union of two soul mates, marriage could actually become a passionate adventure.

In his studio, Glen had a photo album that he kept on a shelf, and when he wasn't around, I would take it down and look at it. The album was filled with photos of him and his wife, Kay, and their exciting life together throughout the years. She had been a concert pianist, while he was an artist-intellectual. Although they never had children, they traveled the world together, carving out a life so rich that it seemed to embody everything I dreamed married life could represent.

They went café hopping in Paris . . . skiing in Gstaad . . . hiking through the Alps . . . antique hunting on Portobello Road. Their adventures were right there in front of my eyes on the tattered pages of the album, where the faded black-and-white photos, tucked carefully into little triangular corners, sprang to life: Glen and Kay with Hemingway, sitting at a little outdoor café in Paris, with their eyes twinkling at some arcane joke; Glen and Kay in Gertrude Stein's salon, lounging on Oriental carpets and plush ottomans side by side with Scott and Zelda Fitzgerald; Glen and Kay flanking Picasso, whose broad arms were draped over their shoulders in a pose so casual I could literally feel the intimacy.

It was a fantasy relationship come to life. Names and faces that I had only read about in history books or seen in *Life* magazine, now became living, breathing people who were interacting with an incredibly intriguing couple. These were flesh-and-blood luminaries who had shared meals, conversations, and excursions with someone I knew, someone who lived right next door.

I looked at Glen's photographs again, and I knew: *This is what I want for myself. This is part of the landscape I want to design for my own marriage.*

Yet, how could I attain it? I was a poor kid from a broken home in a small rural town in California. How could any of these global visions of a great relationship come true?

After high school, Nanette and I drifted apart, seeking independent adventures of our own. I headed for Berkeley and then Los Angeles to study art, while she embarked on studies that would prepare her to be a nurse.

But during these periods of separation, we stayed connected in spirit through the vision of a great marriage that had grasped our imagination years before—and through something else. Certainly, it helped that Nanette and I came to share the same vision of marriage. But even more significant, we came to share the same faith, which provided us with compatible assumptions about ourselves, our children, and the meaning of life.

Now, after more than two decades of marriage and four beautiful children, there is much about that first vision that still proves valid every day. Certainly, we have made plenty of mistakes and found that some of our early ideas about marriage had to be revised or discarded. But as we have trusted that God has the power to intervene and effect beneficial change, we have watched him transform a good two-person relationship into a dynamic and ever-deepening union with a mutual sense of calling and mission.

Seaside Hideaway

THE OLD FISHIN' HOLE

Becoming Like a Child

I regard a good mother to be the ultimate creative professional because if she succeeds, she shapes the most important creation of all—a human life.

Anything I paint on a canvas, or a fine musical composition, or even a marvelous novel written by a Nobel Prize–winning author may have some staying power. But ultimately, such creations are not lasting. If the world blew up tomorrow, my paintings, along with all the world's books, landmark buildings, and inventions, would disappear in the devastation. A child, on the other hand, is eternal.

But is it really possible to "create a child"? Or to put this question another way, how can we best use our imaginations to enhance our ability to rear and relate to our children?

Many people I know are actually afraid of kids—or at least profoundly insecure about their capacity to guide children through the dangerous minefields of life. They may feel more or less comfortable with their own small children. But when those boys and girls reach adolescence, doubts and questions usually arise, even among normally confident, savvy parents. In casual conversations, I often hear such comments as:

"Why didn't I exert more discipline with Johnny when he was in elementary school?"

Or, "I should have made Susie go to church."

Or, "We should never have allowed Heather to watch so much TV."

And if you ask adults to help coach a community sports team, teach a Sunday school class, or otherwise assume a role where they have to supervise and guide young minds and bodies, more often than not, many will run in the opposite direction.

To overcome such fears and misgivings, I would suggest approaching each child on his or her level—in effect, *becoming a child* as you relate to children. Or, to use one of my previous examples, see that kid as a blank canvas. I'm not suggesting that the boy or girl be objectified or depersonalized. Instead, try to view each little one as a *child of God,* poised to be shaped and sculpted in God's image. With this approach, you're more likely to think about your child creatively, apart from the stereotypical adult-child relationship.

To maximize his creativity in working with children, my friend Bill, an award-winning teacher of grammar school kids, has an exercise he calls "wild possibilities." He asks his students, "What's the wildest thing you can imagine yourself doing? What's the wildest thing you want to do?"

When he asked that question of one group of fourth graders, they immediately answered, "Wouldn't it be wild to become pirates and take over a ship?"

In a stroke of creative wizardry, Bill took the next step: He made arrangements for these kids to stage a mock "pirate takeover" of a sailing vessel in San Francisco Bay. Dressed like a motley band straight out of *Treasure Island,* the kids took over the ship's crew by "force," climbed the masts, hoisted the sails, and headed out to sea. It was an adventure none of them would ever forget.

You certainly don't have to take over a pirate ship to fire up your creative passions with the children around you, but it is important to step out boldly in new and maybe even radical directions. Remember that children's book you were always thinking about writing? Perhaps you should pull your child in as a collaborator or even coauthor. I can't think of a better "resource person" for a children's book than a child. And even if the book never gets published, you will have established an entirely new connection with the youngster.

Now, consider that decorating project you've been meaning to begin in your house, but just haven't had time to start. Why not form a committee at home and give the kids significant authority to come up with their own ideas and put them into effect?

One couple I know in Colorado regularly revamps the interior of their home, and each time, they give their three children free rein to choose the colors. Each child gets to pick not only the color of his or her own room, but also the color of another room in the house. A few years back when it was time to redo the paint job, nine-year-old James picked a Granny Smith green for his room, a bright rosy red for the front hallway, and a pistachio green for the living room. His sister, Kathleen, age seven, chose a buttercup yellow for the computer room off the living room and a delicate lavender for her bedroom, while teenage William settled on a China blue for his hideaway.

"It doesn't matter how much the rooms clash," says his dad, Philip, who enlists the help of the kids in doing the painting. "We make it work, and somehow it always looks beautiful."

Now it's time to repaint, and this time Mom got her choice for the hallway: orange!

Of course, such an approach assumes a willingness to let go of some control over the way your house looks. But if you can let go as this family did, you may find that the creative payoff is worth it in family relationships that become closer and richer.

There are other possibilities as well. Maybe you've always wanted to start a Brownie troop for your daughter—in part to give her a whole new circle of friends. Or perhaps you've considered forming a kids' swim team or writing club. Whatever dream you may have conjured up about enhancing your connection with your kids, maybe now is the time to act on that wonderful idea.

COUNTRY MEMORIES

Doing a Dickens

It's not necessary to think in terms of setting up some formal project to achieve successful creative interactions with your kids. Just pulling them into your orbit informally during your daily work and activities may provide them with a helpful model of creativity. Also, sharing your workspace, which they know is extremely important to you, will demonstrate to them how important you think they are—and how much you love them.

In this regard, I'm reminded of an account of how the great novelist Charles Dickens integrated his work into his role as father. Like many of us, he often tended to give his work a top priority, and I know as well as anyone that this kind of intensity may work to shut family members out. The different writing studios Dickens used during his career were designed to promote privacy and isolation. One study was actually situated on the top floor of the house among the treetops.

But even though Dickens was a highly focused writer, he relaxed his work rules now and then to allow his children to enter his writing space. His daughter Mary sometimes crept into his study as he scribbled away in the mornings, laboring at a desk that he always arranged in a precise, familiar way. There, says biographer Wolf Mankowitz in *Dickens of London,* Mary noticed some rather quirky—and entertaining—features of his creative style.

According to observations that Mary recorded later, Dickens frequently hopped up and hurried over to a mirror that he had hung on one wall. Staring at his own reflection, he would contort his face into different expressions in an effort to mimic the looks of one of his characters. At times, he would talk and murmur to himself as he stared, apparently in an effort to re-create just the right dialogue. Then he would return to his desk to record what he had observed and experienced.

Of course, when we become deeply engaged in a creative project, there is always the danger that peaceful, productive family relationships will be placed at risk. Dickens could become so emotionally involved in his work that he actually began to live and feel as his characters lived and felt. In those states, it was sometimes hard for him to be the ideal father.

When he was writing *A Christmas Carol* in the fall of 1843, for example, he became so consumed by the story that he would alternately cry and laugh as he composed. This charged atmosphere that he created in his working space could carry over in a negative way to his outside encounters with family members. His daughter noted that he might come down for lunch after a particularly intense writing session and be so preoccupied that he would eat mechanically and return to his study without speaking to the family much at all.

But on other occasions, the creative momentum he had established in his study would carry over in a winsome and positive way to his interactions with other family members and friends. His brother-in-law, Henry Burnett, wrote that one night as Dickens's wife, Kate, his sister Fanny, and Burnett were sitting around a fire talking, Charles Dickens burst into the room with a portion of *Oliver Twist*, which he was drafting. He retired to a table in a corner of the room and continued with his writing—but interrupted occasionally with his own contributions to the conversation.

Burnett said, "It was interesting to watch, upon the sly, the mind and the muscles working (or, if you please, *playing*) in company, as new thoughts were being dropped upon the paper. And to note the working brow, the set of mouth, with the tongue rightly pressed against the closed lips, as was his habit" (Mankowitz, 1976, 1977, 69–70).

To achieve such creative synergy—which links creative effort with personal relationships—requires a rather intricate balancing act by a Charles Dickens or anyone else. For inner focus and outward relationships somehow to reach a harmonious equilibrium, several prerequisites seem necessary:

First, the creative person must *prepare emotionally and spiritually* in a secure, familiar space. This harkens back to our discussion of the importance of solitude, inner peace, and the "creative place," which we explored on Day One. As for Dickens, he first had to feel totally comfortable in his private, creative space before he could share with others. He could write in almost any environment *after* the creative impulse had been set loose, but before that could happen, he had to launch the creative effort in his own secure, well-designed space.

When he was on one extended trip to Italy, for instance, he found that he simply couldn't get started with his writing in the mornings, despite the fact that he was in the midst of frescoes by Michelangelo and views over golden fish pools, orange trees, the Genoa harbor, and the Alps in the far distance. In a telling observation, he told a friend that he couldn't compose because he had been "plucked out of [his] proper soil" in London (131).

Second, before admitting children or other family members into the creative process, the creator must *build creative momentum* in a special space. Usually, that means making significant progress on a chosen project, whether a painting, piece of writing, business assignment, or volunteer activity.

Finally, after the creative juices have been really flowing for a reasonable period of time, it may be time to "try a Dickens." That is, open yourself and your work to your family. Certainly, this can be risky because you may find that admitting others—especially unpredictable children—to the creative process breaks your train of concentration. On the other hand, if you have prepared for the event, you may discover that welcoming your children into your work and creative life actually benefits everyone—including you.

Although I usually work in complete privacy and isolation, I can identify with Dickens's interactive creative experiences, and many have been the times when the kids will work on their own creative projects in Dad's studio. In fact, on a few occasions I've allowed my children to take up a brush and paint alongside me, especially during the exuberant "lay-in" phase of work. This often leads to unexpected results (such as the time my daughter Winsor spontaneously began finger painting on the current work in progress!).

Furthermore, when I reflect on my own plein air work, I am amazed at the level of creative interaction I encounter. As I have suggested in another context in this book, I always prepare thoroughly for outdoor painting in the quiet of my studio or when I'm driving around, scoping out possible locales for my work. Then, when I actually set up my easel and begin to draw, block out, and paint, I can easily absorb those personal encounters without missing a creative beat—even on those occasions when all sorts of people, including young children, walk past, look over my shoulder, or engage me in conversation.

When I'm properly prepared and riding a wave of creativity, these interactions usually energize me and, I believe, make my painting more vibrant and connected to the real world. Even more important, when my children become involved in my work, I am able to bring them into the broader orbit of my work life and perhaps teach them a little about the creative passion that drives their dad. But these are principles I had to learn largely on my own—because I lacked a proper model in my own father.

Country Memories

GOLDEN GATE BRIDGE

An Accidental Dad

We parents have more power to influence and shape the minds and moral character of our children than we'll ever know. Those who are around their kids all day long obviously are going to have a huge impact. But at the same time, I'm convinced the greatest influence comes more from what we do in our children's presence—or what we jointly experience with them—than from what we try to teach through verbal advice and ad hoc lectures.

In fact, a parent who isn't around much may make an indelible impression, positive or negative. And those deep impressions, which may well be transmitted unconsciously or accidentally, often last a lifetime. Ironically, I owe part of my great dream in life—my calling as an artist—to my often-absent dad. Furthermore, I'm sure that he was unaware of the impact he was having on me.

As a kid, the one piece of tangible evidence I had of Dad in the house was his artwork. When I was little, I never saw him paint, never even heard him talk about painting. But three or four of his landscapes and seascapes hung on our walls wherever we lived. Oddly enough, despite her anger and frustration, my mother kept these highly personal reminders of my father, even long after her marriage to him was over. From my earliest memory, these paintings graced the walls of our trailer and then of our little house. Every day of my young life, I saw those paintings staring down at me, and at some unconscious level, I suppose, they served as an inspiration.

From them, I came to understand that whatever my dad's failings as a father, whatever his weaknesses as a man, a glimmer of creativity, a spark of the divine lay within him. Although that spark had never exploded into a raging fire, the light was there, inside him and also inside me. I also believed that even if during his wanderings he had managed to douse the flame, I could still keep mine burning.

I suppose it wasn't by accident that I was with my father the day I discovered the power a painting possesses to communicate feelings. When I was around seven, my dad arrived at our door one day and took my brother and me to San Francisco. We went to Fisherman's Wharf, where for some reason he walked me into an art gallery. Aside from the fact that he may have realized I was a creatively obsessed kid who drew all the time, I don't have a clue why he took us there. It seemed so out of character for this crusty World War II veteran to walk into a gallery.

But there we were, surrounded by paintings, and suddenly, looming in front of me, was a painting of the Golden Gate Bridge. In the foreground, waves crashed on the shore, and through the waves streamed shafts of glorious sunlight.

I was mesmerized.

Like someone who can't take his eyes off a magician performing sleight-of-hand tricks, I couldn't stop staring at the scene in front of me. The work was an original oil painting—probably just some cheap tourist art—but it drew me in so completely that I stood riveted to the floor, totally absorbed by the light. I could almost feel the warmth of the sunlight on my arms and the brightness on my face. I was bathed in the emotional light—drenched in it, enveloped in it, as though I were standing onshore by the bridge, inside the painting itself.

My mouth fell open. *How could a human hand craft such a wonder? How was it possible?*

I knew what I could do with pencil and paper—but paint? How could an artist create such a glow with nothing more than a brush and a few dabs of color? The mystery seemed unfathomable, and yet, I wanted desperately to know the answer.

My dad's impatient voice pulled me out of my reveries. "Tommy— let's go!"

As we left the gallery, I straggled behind, looking wistfully over my shoulder. About a half hour later, while Dad and my brother were busy poring over model cable cars and Alcatraz memorabilia in another tourist shop, I heard myself making up an excuse to leave.

"Dad, can I go down the street? I forgot something."

Embarrassed to tell him where I was going, I slipped away and headed straight back to the gallery, where I stood rooted in front of the painting, staring.

Twenty minutes later, my dad came charging through the door, swearing like a marine.

"What in blazes are you doing here?" he asked, actually using language that was slightly more colorful.

I just shrugged. I had caught a vision that couldn't be pushed aside by harsh words. I dreamed about that painting that very night, and the night after that, and the one after that.

As I've thought back on that childhood experience hundreds of times over the past forty years or so, I end up wondering every time: *Who could have put that obsession in a little boy's mind?*

As I matured, an answer finally began to take shape: *It had to be God's divine hand of guidance.*

But then I asked myself, "What vehicle did God use to give me that creative drive?" And at least in part, the answer that keeps returning to me is, *My dad.*

Up to that time in San Francisco, all I had done was draw. I was a cartoonist, a caricature artist. Anything I could imagine, I could draw. That was my knack, my gift. But once I discovered the painting of the Golden Gate Bridge during that outing with Dad, my life took a different turn. Oil painting and the creation of light on canvas became my obsessions.

Dad never gave me a lesson in art or discussed theories of aesthetics. Despite those paintings on our walls, I never considered that he and I might be connected through a love of artistic expression. Yet, somehow, his buried artistic urges were transmitted to me.

For the next ten years, an overwhelming compulsion drove me to learn everything I could about how to create a painting—how to execute the brushwork, the composition, the perspective, the light, and the shade. In short, I was obsessed with absorbing everything there was to know about how to become a painter.

I didn't buy my first set of oil paints until I was twelve because tubes of paint were expensive and I couldn't afford them. Nonetheless, every waking moment, I steeped myself in the art of oil painting—by reading, studying, and thinking about it. It was as if I were in a dream as I tweaked and explored this calling of mine. Soon, the dream wasn't shrouded in haze or mist. It grew clearer day by day, and year by year—as clear as the sun shining through those waves in the painting of the Golden Gate Bridge.

Ever since that experience, I have never taken my contacts with my children for granted—and I have advised others to take care as well in those relationships. Just as my absent father "accidentally" exerted a profound influence on my life, I know that I, too, am shaping the lives of my kids in unseen, unknown ways. So I always try to watch my children closely for emerging interests and talents. Then, when I identify a particular trait or passion, I search for opportunities and experiences that may help the child fan the flames of that passion into a creative firestorm.

Finally, especially in families that have been racked by divorce or separation, it is always exciting for a parent and child to complete the circle from accidental or unknown influences to a conscious agape love relationship. For years I had yearned to draw closer to my dad, but I could never quite figure out how to reconnect. We saw each other occasionally, but it was never long enough to get to know each other man-to-man.

Then one day, while I was in the familiar, relatively undemanding final phase of painting a rustic mountain scene in my art series *The End of a Perfect Day,* I had a breakthrough thought: *Why not bring Dad into the studio for an extended conversation?*

Dad was willing, and so I set up a rocking chair in my studio, turned on a tape recorder, and started plying him with questions about his exploits during World War II. I painted, and he talked—and talked, and talked. It was better than therapy for both of us.

Over a series of weeks, he reminisced about the war, about mistakes he had made and about regrets that he had. Day by day, this eighty-one-year-old man and his forty-something son developed a bond. We became so close that I came up with another brainstorm:

"Let's go to Europe and revisit the beach where you landed at Normandy and see the other places you experienced during the war!" I exclaimed. A few months later, my brother, Pat, and I bundled up Dad for the biggest road trip for our lives.

But I think the best way I discovered for completing the circle of that father-son relationship was to challenge him to take up a brush and canvas and start painting again. There had always been a strain of artistic talent in the family: My grandfather, a professional moonshiner in the Ozarks during Prohibition, was also an engraver for newspaper art and illustrations. My dad had taken the skill a step or two further by creating his own paintings when he was a young adult. But then he had dropped his art as the years went on and family responsibilities grew.

Wanting to deepen my relationship with him in his twilight years, I asked, "Dad, why don't you take up painting again?"

"Nah, I couldn't paint," he replied.

"I'll do you one better," I said in a moment that I can attribute only to divine inspiration. "I'll be your patron. Any painting you do, I'll buy it—for $300 a painting."

Because he was financially strapped—and also because that creative spark was still present—he didn't hesitate: "You're on!" he said.

So he started churning out paintings, sometimes three or four a month—mostly landscapes. My collection now contains almost sixty paintings done by my dad in his last years. I fully expect that one day, they'll be hanging next to my own—perhaps even in a future museum show. In return, he was able to feel good about earning some extra funds in the final years of his life, as he employed a skill he truly enjoyed. In fact, one of the last things he said to me just before his death was, "I've got to go home and get back to my easel."

My interactions with my father—and his impact on me—may have begun as seemingly random, accidental influences, which neither he nor I understood at first. But I think both of us finally comprehended, at least to some degree, the truth that "accidental" family relationships are not really accidents at all, but rather, purposeful events in a broader fabric of life.

The challenge for all of us is to wend our way through the debris that may litter parent-child relationships, find the buried gold nuggets, and then celebrate them before our time together is gone. Fortunately, by the end of his life, Dad and I were able to transform those earlier unplanned influences into an intentional—and highly rewarding—father-son bond.

Lamplight Bridge

Finding a True Friend

Better is a neighbor nearby than a brother far away" (Prov. 27:10, NKJV). That ancient saying has always summed up the essence of true friendship for me.

Throughout my life, real friends have always been extremely important to me, close to the status of full family members. Many have sustained and shaped my life when family members simply weren't available: people like my neighbor-artist, Glen Wessels; my "hobo" travel companion, Jim Gurney; business associates; gallery owners; and countless others. Without these support troops, my creative efforts would most likely have fallen flat—because, as we pursue new ideas and insights, we all need close human companions to affirm us and serve as our sounding boards.

In fact, for many the only real "family" and "advisory board" to help sort through important issues and make life-shaping decisions is a network of valued friends. These people who are part of one's inner circle listen to daily complaints, provide wise advice for the future, encourage us in times of failure or rejection, and rejoice in the wake of our victories and achievements.

What constitutes a true friend? Several bedrock tests come to mind.

First, *a true friend should be available*—even when time constraints, a busy schedule, or distance threatens to get in the way. Many times, a seeming friend may consistently give work pressures or other interests a priority over personal relationships. When that happens, the person becomes more an acquaintance than a true friend. Conversely, a friend can be "nearby," in the sense of the proverb quoted above, even when he is living a thousand or more miles away—provided both parties make a serious effort to keep personal connections open and vital.

I'm reminded of one man—call him Ivan—who often would complain when one of his close friends had to move out of town. "Well, that's the end of that friendship," he would say.

Ivan thought he was just being realistic, and it is quite true that when a person moves to another part of the country, old friendships may be neglected as fresh personal ties arise in the new location. But when Ivan himself moved to a new city, he discovered e-mail and the strategic telephone call—and realized that he didn't have to be next door to maintain a vital, close friendship.

By using e-mail to send personal pictures, pertinent news articles, and short, thoughtful messages to several friends at his old location, he discovered that he could actually *enhance* those relationships. Many times, his missives, which required some thought and reflection, focused on issues that he might have overlooked during casual lunches or other outings. In return, his friends gave him valuable advice, either through e-mail or over the phone, which often helped him make difficult decisions at his new job or in new relationships. Paradoxically, the increased distance made it possible for him to be "nearby" his old friends in unexpected, highly creative ways he had never anticipated or experienced before.

Second, *a true friend should be able to celebrate without envy in times of success.* Now, this is an extremely rare quality in a friend. Sometimes, people will celebrate with you because they sense they have something to gain. Other times, they will *appear* to celebrate, but deep inside they harbor reservations, resentments, and envy.

I think that the tenth commandment, "You shall not covet . . . anything that is your neighbor's" expresses not only a rule for dealing with possessions, but also a profound insight into envious human nature and psychology. Maybe God was tipping us off that he knows how hard it is for us to rejoice in the good fortune of others—even those we say are our best friends. But until we reach the point where we really can celebrate the success of others, we'll never know true friendship. And until we find a friend who celebrates without reservation with us, we'll lack a committed companion and collaborator who will be eager and willing to help us progress to the next stage in our creative efforts.

Third, *a true friend should provide genuine support in times of trouble*—and not merely turn into a finger-pointer or faultfinder. On one level, this means guarding against the error of Job's friends, who made quite logical arguments about Job's possible faults, but lacked the grace and capacity to sit quietly with him, empathizing and bearing his burdens in prayer.

Even worse, too many of us may be inclined to slip into the outlook identified by the seventeenth-century French intellectual and author La Rochefoucauld, who observed, "In the misfortune of our best friends we often find something that is not displeasing." Expanding on La Rochefoucauld's maxim, the eighteenth-century British writer Jonathan Swift wrote that "in all distresses of our friends / We first consult our private ends."

Think about this point for a moment. Your first response may be, "Oh, I never feel that way!" But in fact, at one time or another, most of us have felt some satisfaction—or perhaps mild relief—when an extremely successful friend has run into trouble in his or her upward ascent in life.

Maybe the friend has made a lot more money than you, but has had some financial reversals on the stock market. Or maybe the parents you know with the perfect, high-achieving children now have an offspring who has not quite lived up to expectations. Or perhaps the slightly arrogant leader in your business or volunteer organization, who has always been chosen the head of committees or departments, has stumbled and lost her position of authority. These are the situations that the words of La Rochefoucauld, Swift, and other insightful thinkers may bring to mind as we ponder the nature of true friendship—the kind that provides a platform for great personal creativity.

These essentials of true friendship—availability, celebration, and support in tough times—characterized the friendship network of the nineteenth-century French Master caricaturist Honoré Daumier. But ironically, Daumier wasn't the kind of man you would automatically associate with a wide and deep network of friends.

He would typically wander around on his own, in and out of the side streets and shops of Paris, hunting subjects for his paintings. Or he would spend solitary hours in an artistic eyrie, an isolated attic room high over the waters of the Seine, where he watched workhorses and fishermen along the banks. Or he would study floating bathhouses littered with unclothed patrons who were candidates for the caricaturist's pen.

Then, when he had absorbed sufficient shapes and colors from the outside to form his inner mental vision, he retired to perform the bulk of creation in his specially appointed attic studio. His workspace featured bare walls punctuated by a couple of prints in the style of Delacroix. In the center of the room, he placed an easel, which was usually occupied by some work in progress. Other stacked canvases and panels lay against the walls, and a stand-alone iron stove provided heating on cold days. All in all, his quarters and personality didn't seem overly compatible with gregarious get-togethers with friends. In fact, historian Oliver Larkin in *Daumier: Man of His Time* described him as a "semi-recluse" (1966, 81).

Yet despite Daumier's extreme penchant for privacy—a trait that most creative people cultivate to one extent or another—he was happy to welcome friends into his creative space at irregular intervals. And they were consistently the kind of friends who lent support and help to Daumier's creative efforts.

For example, his fellow painter Courbet, who might have seemed a prime candidate to become the caricaturist's competitor, actually pushed him to submit a sketch for a competition, which promised to raise his artistic profile. Another friend, the novelist and journalist Jules Champfleury, shored up Daumier's self-esteem and confidence by emphasizing that the art of caricature, often regarded in the Paris salons as inferior, was an ideal vehicle to communicate the plight of the common man. Both Champfleury and Daumier participated in the bohemian lifestyle of Paris that attracted many artists and writers of the day. Another frequent visitor to his spare attic studio was the writer Charles Baudelaire, who kept Daumier on his toes in scintillating discussions and also built him up in published essays that compared him to great masters like Delacroix and Ingres.

So even though the bulk of Daumier's creative work occurred in solitude, in his private space he intuitively understood how essential it was for a creative person to maintain true friendships. They not only nurtured him emotionally and philosophically, but also contributed to his reputation and success as an artist.

So don't be shy—let your friends in on the creative process. Norman Rockwell was famous for showing works in progress to milkmen, delivery boys, and any casual friend that happened by his studio. He gathered strength and creativity from their idle comments and input. So open up! Set aside any insecurity you may feel about your talents and share your creative projects with those you know. Read that poem aloud for friends at a dinner party; raise your voice in song at the next karaoke microphone you encounter; e-mail your short story or photos of your watercolor paintings to a few old acquaintances. You'll probably be pleasantly surprised at the responses you get. And you will definitely be encouraged to further develop your creative habit.

Creativity is at heart a reflection of life. And friends and loved ones are necessary to provide the vitality and inspiration we need to realize our full creative potential.

A Quiet Evening

Living in Love

Agape love is a pervasive thread that binds personal creativity into one powerful, focused package. Without such love, the creative impulse can become ineffectual or irrelevant, or move into destructive channels of expression.

Consider, for instance, how creative—yet negative and even harmful—some contemporary music, films, and TV programs can be as they manipulate and extol violence, uncontrolled sex, or other immoral conduct. Then, reflect on how different our culture might be if agape love replaced all these creative distortions. In a sense, then, it's accurate to say that we have been designed to *live in love* even as we engage in acts of creativity.

As you prepare to place love more at the center of your life, it may be helpful to keep in mind three fundamental imperatives that summon us to love more expansively, creatively, and passionately.

Love Expansively—but Wisely

On this third day of creative living, we have seen that the noblest form of love, the agape love that originates in God himself, encompasses everyone with whom we come in contact—spouses, children, parents, siblings, friends, business colleagues, and casual acquaintances.

But even though we are called to love them all, we know that we can't devote the same amount of time to each person we encounter, and sometimes that can generate some frustrations or guilt feelings. How often have you fretted when you simply didn't have time to have friends over for dinner, or had to miss some special party, or couldn't attend a particular family function?

I'm constantly confronting such second thoughts and misgivings in my own life because although so many nice people regularly cross my path, I simply can't find enough minutes in the day to relate to them all as I'd like. But I manage to keep guilt and anxiety at bay by keeping in mind, first of all, that while I want to love expansively—touching everyone I have the power to touch—I have my limits. So I must choose wisely the ones with whom I'll spend most of my waking hours.

To make wise love choices, it helps me to view my relationships as a pattern of concentric circles, with the closest friends and family members in the inner circle or two, and the casual acquaintances in the outer bands. Although the outer circles may include hundreds of people, the inner bands have room for a relatively small number of individuals, say six to twelve. There just isn't enough time in the day for me to relate with any quality to more people than that.

As a guide, I sometimes refer to Jesus, who chose twelve—plus a few other friends such as Lazarus, Mary, and Martha—for his in-depth relationships. And when it came to special events, trips, and conversations, such as the Transfiguration and many healings, the number actually decreased to only three—Peter, James, and John. I figure that if Christ felt he had to limit his very close friendships to that extent, I shouldn't worry if I find that time constraints demand I do the same.

Love Creatively

Even the closest relationships can become stale if we fail to approach them creatively. For example, doing the same things over and over again with your spouse will inevitably threaten to turn the marriage into a humdrum routine, with little or no spice and verve.

One couple I know found a rather creative way to overcome the threat of monotony and tedium: They resurrected an activity that had drawn them together during their courtship—the love of ballroom dancing. Although they had continued to dance infrequently over the years, they found that once or twice a year just wasn't enough to keep up their skills and recapture the old fun and excitement.

So when a professional ballroom dance studio opened in their town, they signed up for the Argentine tango. Learning the basics of the smooth, eight-step Latin dance changed their marriage. The husband woke up many mornings visualizing the new steps they had learned the night before—perhaps a "tango waltz" variation or a "blocking" movement that required his wife to step high over his outstretched leg.

As for the wife, she began to collect swirling dresses and costume jewelry with a South American flourish and flavor. The deep looks they learned to give each other on the dance floor carried over to dinner . . . and dessert . . . and, well, you get the picture. Anyhow, the message in their experience is that love demands creativity, just as creativity demands love.

Make Love Your Passion

Ultimately, agape love should drive *every* successful creative endeavor; it must become the passion that surpasses all other passions. When you become immersed in a work assignment, a volunteer project, or any other activity—but you lack love in your life—your creative aspirations will become out of balance.

One of the most poignant and telling little stories I've encountered in this regard involved Vicki Rose, a popular speaker to women's groups in south Florida. The demand for Vicki's services escalated, and she found she had to spend a great deal of time away from home at night and on weekends. At first, this increase in her workload seemed appropriate to Vicki; after all, she was following a personal passion that was contributing to the lives of many women.

But a creative passion can be a complex phenomenon when that passion touches important personal relationships. As it happened, Vicki's daughter, Courtney, was a senior in high school at the time and was preparing to leave for college. The impending separation made the girl more conscious that this might be the last time she and her mother would be able to spend significant amounts of time together.

But Vicki, who was so consumed by her speaking responsibilities, remained relatively unaware of these feelings—until her daughter finally said, "Mom, can you stop doing all you're doing and spend some time with me?"

Those direct words abruptly jerked Vicki back on track. She immediately recognized that, sure, her speaking engagements were important. But her daughter—especially at this significant juncture in life—was more important. And so, with the exception of two local talks, Vicki abruptly quit everything she was doing. For the next eight months, until Courtney entered college, she remained totally available to her daughter. Through this precious gift of time, she affirmed that her love for Courtney was a passion that took precedence over any job.

Interestingly, however, the story continues because Vicki's experience and insight have become an object lesson that she shares regularly with the women in her audiences. Her agape creativity has even reached the pages of this book, and—who knows?—may even benefit you.

THE FOURTH DAY
OF CREATIVE LIVING

The Call to Community

We have learned to be citizens of the world,
members of the human community.

— FRANKLIN DELANO ROOSEVELT,
FOURTH TERM INAUGURAL ADDRESS, JANUARY 20, 1945

VENICE

The World Beyond

Most of us limit our world to those we know, to the associates and acquaintances who are most familiar to us. We try to carve out time in our busy schedules for friends and loved ones, but when it comes to strangers, well, that's another matter. More often than we would probably like to admit, we have a tribal rather than a global outlook on our relationship with outsiders.

For example, few of us are as willing as Jesus often was to put off a holiday, a vacation, or even a short time of rest in order to respond to the needs of strangers. One wonders about the possibly rattled or annoyed reaction of his disciples when he told them, "Come aside by yourselves to a deserted place and rest a while"—but then immediately postponed the holiday when he was pressed to teach and feed the five thousand (Mark 6:31ff. NKJV).

Regardless of how disagreeable or inconvenient such interruptions by strangers may seem at the time, I believe that we are called to be creative in the wide world beyond our limited homes or neighborhoods. In fact, I question whether it's even possible to be truly creative—and exert the greatest possible influence on the public through our particular gifts and efforts—if we lack a broad perspective on our personal passions.

In *The Hobbit,* the precursor to his great trilogy *The Lord of the Rings,* J. R. R. Tolkien suggested an interesting twist on some of these ideas about strangers and creativity and great achievements in the world. In describing different types of hobbits—the small, humanlike creatures who inhabited his fantasies—Tolkien said that the "Baggins" line "never had any adventures or did anything unexpected" while the "Took" family "would go and have adventures" in lands far from home (see "Selected References," Tolkien 1966, 1, 2). As it happened in *The Hobbit,* the mother of Tolkien's hero, Bilbo Baggins, was a Took, and fortunately, the Took strain won out. Baggins embarked on a great adventure and set in motion a series of events that eventually saved the earth.

Now, I'm not suggesting that if you broaden your perspective and allow your creativity to reach beyond your narrow circle of friends and family, you'll automatically change the world. But it's almost a certainty that if you limit your outreach and influence to your backyard, you'll have an impact on only your backyard.

In fact, restricting personal creativity can have an even more serious impact on personalities and character. I've discovered there is no such thing as creativity that stands still. Either you move forward, or you retreat; you progress, or you lose ground; you intensify, or you stultify.

A prime illustration of this principle is the phenomenon of human aging. Among preventive medicine specialists—including Dr. Kenneth H. Cooper, founder of the Cooper Clinic and Cooper Institute in Dallas and inventor of aerobics, according to the *Encyclopaedia Britannica*—it's an established fact that as you grow older, you steadily lose muscle and bone mass. Yet it's possible to retard or even reverse this steady deterioration with a systematic program of weight-bearing exercise. In other words, from a physical perspective, human beings can't just stand still. If they decide to do nothing, the body grows weaker; but if they engage in regular exercise, they may even become stronger than they were in their youth.

It's similar with creativity. Those who fail to exercise their creative gifts to the maximum can expect the creative spark and passion to grow dim. And those who neglect creative faculties and impulses entirely will find that personal creativity shrivels and may even die.

So on this Fourth Day of Creative Living, let's prepare to expand and strengthen the creative impulse with a few unsettling adventures. We'll begin on a small scale, looking at family roots and hometowns. Then, we'll open ourselves to a little unsettling serendipity—unexpected happenings and people that can enrich life immeasurably. Finally, we'll reach far beyond our city limits to events and situations that have the power to touch our deepest emotions and also may change our lives.

Venice

HOMETOWN MORNING

Links to the Past

The most powerful creative impulses are those that are firmly rooted in our own personal histories. Or to put this another way, creativity doesn't grow in a vacuum; rather, it blooms in a broader context of experience and heritage.

Also, our capacity to be creative is directly related to our grasp of present and past events, people, and cultures. Reflect for a moment on how this principle might play out for you in practice:

- You can't generate useful ideas for a business if you haven't had some experience with that company's past operations;
- You're unlikely to contribute brilliant insights to a service or religious group unless you understand something about that group's history, organization, or mission;
- You can't write meaningfully about a culture you don't understand or have failed to research; and
- You can't paint with any authenticity scenes you've never witnessed or at least fathomed or visualized in detail in your imagination.

As we nurture our personal creative capacities, then, it's imperative that we explore and exploit our broader community context. But that's not always so easy. It's often an uncomfortable or forbidding prospect to reach out to unfamiliar people. In fact, the idea of investigating unknown situations or circumstances can be terrifying.

To deal with these inner barriers, I often advise those seeking greater creativity to start their exploration of the world beyond themselves with contexts and environments close to home. In fact, you don't even have to leave home—just make an effort to learn a little more about your family, neighborhood, and local culture. By connecting with your roots, you'll automatically start posing broader and broader questions that will enhance your creativity in dealing with your family, local community organizations, or even your business.

For example, you might start by asking:

— "How did my family end up in this town?"
— "What was this town like before my family moved here?"
— "How has my home environment influenced me as a person?"
— "How did I end up in this church or synagogue or mosque?"
— "Where did my forebears come from originally?"
— "When did they come to America?"
— "What is it about my ancestry, both here and abroad, that may have made me the person I am today?"

You can see where this is going: To understand your context, it's necessary to formulate *specific* and *pointed* questions about your background and roots, which can throw light on why you're involved in a particular volunteer organization, business enterprise, faith group, or hobby.

You might even try grilling yourself as though you were *both* a news reporter interested in your creative life *and* the interview subject providing the facts and responses. Regardless of the specific questions you come up with, the deeper you get into this kind of personal research, the more fun and fascinating it usually becomes.

To help you get started, here's an illustration of how I might interview myself in an effort to draw out important personal tendencies and facts that may tell me something about my own creative urges.

Q: Thom, why bother asking yourself creativity-related questions about your back-ground—don't you already know yourself pretty well?

A: Actually, I'm constantly amazed at how often new facts and insights about myself emerge when I conduct this kind of self-interview. So I periodically set aside time to reflect on my personal history, such as how my own hometown has influenced me. The more I dig, the more I understand how those early influences have turned me into the Thomas Kinkade of the present.

Q: Okay, so tell me about the accidents of your childhood and early life.

A: I don't assume that any part of my life involved accidents. For example, I don't think it was any accident that I was raised in Placerville, California, in the heart of El Dorado County. In that humble place smack in the middle of Gold Rush country, I found my first nuggets of creative inspiration—nuggets I still think about today as I'm painting various scenes in my study.

Q: What's so special about Placerville?

A: The town—nicknamed "Hangtown" for the infamous hanging judge who once ruled those parts—owes its present name to the gold-containing deposits of sand and gravel found in its riverbeds in the late 1840s. The Spanish called those deposits *placer,* and during the Gold Rush, prospectors flooded the area to pan for gold in a process known as "placer mining."

As I was growing up, reminders of those prospectors cropped up everywhere—from my history textbooks to the foundations of nearby Sutter's Mill, where gold was first discovered. It didn't take much for me to imagine myself back there with them in a tent-strewn mining camp on the parched hills of Hangtown, getting ready for a hard day's work.

Q: So reflecting on the history of Hangtown gets your imagination churning?

A: Yep. I can picture those early adventurers even now. With nothing but a shovel and a simple steel pan blackened over a campfire to contrast with any gold flakes he might find, a miner would head for the hills or a nearby riverbed to strike it rich. His task was simple but laborious. Filling his pan with placer, the prospector would thrust the pan under water and rotate it gently in a circular fashion to separate the sand and gravel from the bits of gold. He knew that little by little, if he was patient enough, the lightweight sand and gravel would rise to the top, while any gold would settle to the bottom.

To get closer to his golden prize, the miner periodically tilted his pan ever so carefully to wash away the loose sand and gravel. Then he would repeat the swirling and tilting process—for hours and even days, until nothing was left in the pan but a layer of dark minerals.

Q: Tell me, Thom, do I hear echoes of your own artistic imagination here?

A: Yes, I think you do. As I'm pursuing my own creative work, trying to discover just the right shapes, color combinations, and light intensities, I'm reminded of an early prospector around Placerville. If he was attentive and lucky enough, he might discover a few tiny gold nuggets gleaming among traces of platinum and tin. But I have a few advantages over that early guy. If he wasn't so lucky, he might end up at the wrong end of a barroom brawl or swinging at the end of a rope on "Hangman's Tree" in the center of town.

The Gold Rush captured the creative fancy of thousands of fortune hunters from around the world, who in five years, from 1848 to 1853, swelled California's population from 14,000 to 223,000. Along the way, some of these dreamers managed to unearth more than 125 million ounces of gold, worth $50 billion by today's calculations.

Q: Of course, that early environment—which contained your roots—has changed considerably, hasn't it?

A: True. By the time I came along, the only gold was in the glitzy casinos in nearby Lake Tahoe, and Placerville was just a gas-stop on Route 50. But deep in my own psyche, the aura of adventure and the Gold Rush spirit have still lingered.

As a kid, I felt it every time I went downtown, where a saloon known as "The Hangman's Tree" marked the site of the grisly hangings. Jutting from the front of the establishment, a big old limb from the original tree dangled a life-size effigy of some poor old miner swinging by his neck from a rope. The saloon and the limb and the hanging body are still there—right on Main Street. (Coincidentally, they are right across the street from the very first Thomas Kinkade Gallery ever opened—but I'm getting ahead of myself.)

The whole scene seems kind of morbid when I think of it now, but it was part of the culture I was raised in—a Wild West, risk-taking kind of culture that said, "Anything goes!" It was probably this culture that fostered my own willingness to take a flier on the great creative passion of my life—landscape art.

Q: Your early memories seem quite vivid.

A: Yes, the culture of Placerville got into my bones and fed my imagination, especially at times like the "Wagon Train Days," an annual re-creation of the wagon train that carried the Silver Lode from Lake Tahoe to the coast. After silver was discovered in Nevada in the late 1850s, there was only one trail west to carry the lode over the High Sierra, and it ran straight through Placerville.

Every year as I was growing up, a train of fifty Conestoga wagons traversed the route from Tahoe along what is now Route 50 to celebrate this piece of California history. The drive took a week or more, and the minute the wagon train hit Placerville, the entire town came to a halt. Cops diverted traffic, shops shut down, and schools closed as Placerville got ready for the big parade.

The night before the parade—like every other kid in town—I ran down to the field where the wagons had circled and watched as men and women dressed in old-time western costumes prepared meals over an open fire and then crawled into their wagons to sleep.

I drank in the whole scene—the horse-drawn carriages, the huge Conestoga wagons creaking and swaying as they rumbled down Main Street, and the joy on the faces of neighbors and strangers alike. Along the parade route, the electricity was palpable as people shared doughnuts, swapped gossip, and waved little flags imprinted with the California emblem. As I watched the exuberant crowd and listened to their cheers, I grew nostalgic for a place and time I knew only in my imagination.

Q: Many have said that your paintings evoke deep-rooted longings or memories for such a secure, safe time, when families and personal values were strong and our outlook on the future was optimistic.

A: I think that's true to some extent—though I believe it's important to be realistic about those earlier days. After all, plenty of bad as well as good things went on in the past.

When the wagon train was in town, for instance, a group known as the "Clampers" appeared on the scene to stage a mock hanging. The Clampers, otherwise known as *E Clampus Vitas,* were—and still are—a drinking club for men who get their kicks out of reenacting western traditions. *Rowdy* western traditions. To put it bluntly, the group can best be described as the Elks gone haywire.

One particular year, when I was about eight, the Clampers arrived in Placerville in full western regalia: smelly shirts, dog-eared hats, tattered pants, and scruffy leather boots. Their goal: to "hang" a man wanted for robbery and murder.

I was standing on Main Street just after the parade when the Clampers, brandishing pistols and shouting like banshees, swarmed down the street toward the courthouse steps. Fascinated by this motley collection of humanity, I slipped unseen into the courthouse and hid behind a pillar. Within minutes, the scene got ugly.

"Arrest that man!" someone shouted, pointing to a slight-looking fellow with a leather vest. "He's wanted for murder in Sacramento!" With that, a few burly men grabbed the bewildered man and cuffed his hands behind his back.

"Hang him!" shouted a man in back. "String him up," another retorted.

I watched bug-eyed as someone slipped a noose around the man's neck and threw the other end of the rope over an improvised scaffold. Within seconds, the area erupted in gunshots and epithets as the drunken crowd surged toward the "criminal," chanting, "Hang him! Hang him!"

I was scared out of my wits. But I couldn't move. In my eight-year-old mind, fantasy and reality merged as my history books and the old hangman's tree sprang to life. I wondered: *Are they really going to hang him? Am I back in Hangtown?*

Then a light flashed behind me, and I turned to see a very sixties-looking photographer adjusting his flashbulb.

"Hi, kid," he said. "Look for this in the paper tomorrow."

Sure enough, the next day, my mom walked into the kitchen and handed me a newspaper. Dominating the front page was a three-quarter-page photograph of the Clampers' "hanging." In the foreground, upstaging the unruly mob, sat a kid with a sailor cap on his head. He bore a startling resemblance to me.

The headline said it all: "Re-creating History—Almost." I guess the "almost" referred to the little boy in the foreground.

Q: Even if that reminder of the brutal reality of the past scared you, it sounds like delving into your heritage was a mostly positive exercise.

A: I think it was. From such experiences in an unassuming western town called Placerville, my creativity ran rampant. In that place once known as "Hangtown," I stood on the shoulders of those hope-filled Gold Rush prospectors, dreaming impossible dreams of my own El Dorado. With nothing but the sand and gravel of the Sierra foothills under my feet, I discovered that I could pan for the richest gold of all—the gold of my creative imagination—and paint a canvas as big as my imagination could make it.

New York, Fifth Avenue

The Creative Present

To take full advantage of your "creative present"—the highly stimulating forces that are lurking out there just beyond your front steps—it's absolutely necessary to get involved in the life of your community.

Oh, I've heard most of the objections—and must admit that I've conjured them up myself on occasion:

- "I don't have time to get involved with becoming a mentor for neglected children."
- "I contribute to organizations that help the homeless—so there's no reason for me to devote my valuable time to actually working with them."
- "If I get involved in the church outreach committee, I'll get pulled into church politics—and I certainly don't need that kind of stress."
- "I know the Salvation Army does nice things around our community, but there are plenty of people who like to ring those bells at Christmastime—they don't need me."

In fact, these community programs do need you because there aren't nearly enough volunteers to enable them to maximize their services. But believe it or not, you need your community more than it needs you—especially if you hope to realize your full creative potential.

First of all, greater community involvement will provide you with a more expansive view of the world around you. You'll find that when you're brainstorming about a business issue, you may recall something you learned or heard from a fellow volunteer while you were working on that roof with Habitat for Humanity. Or if you're advising a friend about ways to make his family a closer-knit unit, you may remember how your own family life was enriched when you trooped off together to the local mission to serve a Thanksgiving meal to the homeless.

I have often experienced surges of imagination and creativity that I know didn't just "turn on" the minute I stepped in front of my easel, like some wall switch that I flick on and off. Instead, the creative process may have actually begun far in advance, during an encounter with some community group or activist.

On one occasion, for instance, the president of our local Rotary Club invited me to paint a portrait of my current hometown in California's Santa Cruz mountains as a fund-raiser for children's charities. Now, it would have been easy for me to say no, with the excuse that I was just too busy. But I've had enough positive experiences in such projects that I knew better—so my Rotary Club friend and I did some creative huddling.

The idea was to come up with a painting that would capture the spirit of the town in such a way that everyone—from businessmen to tourists— would want copies of the prints. The way my friend and I had envisioned it, the print would not only jump-start the new breakfast Rotary Club, but also call attention to the needs of kids in our area.

For weeks, creativity bubbled behind the scenes as we explored how this painting would be marketed. I had spent hours in meetings with Rotary Club officers and other community leaders discussing the painting's subject and style. Finally, we opted for a plein air painting, done on location rather than in my studio, in order to reflect the active, free-spirited nature of the town and its people.

Once the style was chosen, it was up to me to find the subject. I had in my mind the idea of painting the "town view"—not just any town view, but a quintessential spot that would reflect the essence of the place. But how would I find it? As I often do, I hopped on my motor scooter for inspiration. I find the freedom and spontaneity intoxicating, so intoxicating that whenever I need new ideas, I seek out the world in the open air. This time was no different.

As I scooted around town, I saw this subject and that. Ahead of me I spotted one scene I thought would be ideal, but then something urged me to keep driving.

When I unleash my imagination in such a project, I never assume that it's entirely up to me. God is always involved in my creative projects, so I prayed, *Lord, what do you have around the corner?*

As I explored farther, I came upon two or three spots that seemed to be possibilities. There was the old plaza, which is considered a town landmark; the park, where families gathered in the evenings; and the rows of perfectly appointed Victorian houses lush with rose gardens on Tait Avenue. But still, none of these views seemed quite right, and so I gunned my cycle and drove on.

I had just rounded the corner onto the main street of town when suddenly it hit me: The best view of town was the classic view, Main Street itself! But even then I was ambivalent. From my vantage point on the east side of the street, I looked squarely at the shops across the way. But my intuition told me, *This isn't it. Go across the street and take a look.*

I followed my inner voice and went across the street, just north of the old art deco theater. There, for the first time, I saw that scene in all its beauty: the rows of restaurants and shops with their neat little awnings; the light posts and eucalyptus trees lining the sidewalk; the cars flanking the curb; and especially the theater, with its bold vertical marquee emblazoned with the town's name stretching toward the sky.

The scene I had taken for granted so many times now came alive in a new way. I had seen it day after day for the last decade, driving downtown for a bite of breakfast at the local coffee shop, or popping into the rural supply shop with Nanette for some gadget for the kitchen. The perfect view had been there all the time, but somehow, I had missed it.

I couldn't help smiling to myself. Wasn't this just like my own life? I see the same scenes, the same circumstances, over and over without any hint of change. I may think about them, obsess on them, rumble over them in my mind, and yet nothing coalesces. But then comes that moment of creative inspiration when the problem is solved, the relationship is fixed, the family difficulty is overcome.

God's currency for making major changes in our lives is creativity— and that's what God poured into my spirit that day: fresh eyes on the same circumstances. As I looked at the facade of the theater, the old marquee suddenly became the town itself. Standing resolutely against the sky, it seemed to symbolize the spiritual center of local life just as the church steeple once did in New England villages.

In my mind's eye, I could picture the way the old movie house must have looked in the forties, when homecoming soldiers would stream into it with their girlfriends, buy a bag of popcorn, and settle into the back seats, smooching and whispering, without paying much attention to the movie.

I could see them all as vividly as if I were sitting right next to them. I saw little boys pocketing the quarters given by their parents, sneaking past the ushers and getting in for free. I saw the ushers with their flashlights, the girls with their bobby socks, and the guys with cigarette packs rolled up in their sleeves.

The theater began to vibrate with everything a small town is—everything a small town should be—families and memories and traditions in the making. And I knew I had my view.

But as I motored home on my cycle, I also knew that I had gained much more than just another idea for another painting. Without the first spark of conversation, the follow-up idea sessions, and the eventual committee meetings, I would never have enjoyed this new experience. A creative expression had lain hidden right in front of my eyes for years; yet on my own, I had remained oblivious to the opportunity. But when I opened my mind and spirit to the riches of my own community, I discovered a new vision of reality—and a fresh experience of the creative present.

New York, Fifth Avenue

City by the Bay

Serendipity

Regardless of how much we plan a creative project, surprise encounters with friends or strangers will inevitably shake things up. But more often than not, those "shake-ups" will inure to our benefit, if we can learn to receive and absorb them in the most constructive way.

For example, an unexpected proposal for a new creative project, such as the painting suggested to me by the Rotary Club in the previous section, may surprise us. Or an outside event—such as a trip to some exotic land—may introduce completely new concepts and people that completely transform the way we look at the world. Or we may unexpectedly run into old friends who once again enrich our lives—or perhaps we'll encounter interesting strangers who provide fresh perspectives on our work or relationships.

But for these surprises to work in our lives, we can't automatically be turned off or frightened by them; instead, we must have the capacity to receive, absorb, and enjoy. This quality of being able to discover and benefit from unsought, unexpected things in life is known as *serendipity*—an interesting word with a long, rich history. The eighteenth-century English writer Horace Walpole was really the one who gave us the term. He was inspired by the Persian fairy tale "The Three Princes of Serendip," whose prince-protagonists had the innate capacity to find wonderful blessings and insights, though seemingly by accident.

I believe each of us experiences serendipity—but few of us know how to reap its optimum benefits. To sharpen and sensitize this special faculty in your own life, you might begin by doing something completely different. This coming weekend, for instance, don't just slip into your usual routine, whether it's a golf or tennis game, work in the yard, or the regular neighborhood card party.

Instead, try a new restaurant, or invite over new acquaintances you've been meaning to entertain, or take a weekend trip out of town, preferably to some location you've never visited. If you shake up your weekend and allow for the possibility of some surprises in your life, I guarantee you'll begin to discover the excitement of serendipity.

Throughout my life, I've cultivated my own sense of serendipity by hitting the highway. I'm passionate about road trips, perhaps because the relatively little time I spent as a child with my dad usually involved outings in his automobile. Our best times were those when he would pack up my brother, Pat, and me and take us in the car to some faraway place like Disneyland. To a couple of kids from northern California, that was like going to a foreign country. Once we even got as far as Rosarita, Mexico, a one-horse town just over the border that was as exciting to me as if we had gone to Machu Picchu. I can still taste the fresh tortillas, see the dancing senoritas, and hear sounds of the mariachi band at the hotel. Those trips were liberating adventures that gave my brother and me a chance to be wild and free.

Ever since those childhood adventures, I've had a hankering to cut loose from the humdrum of daily life—because I have learned from experience that unexpected treasures lie around practically every corner. That's what happened when I was working on one plein air canvas recently. I looked up from my painting to see two burly young men who looked to be in their thirties standing at a respectful distance. At first, they seemed merely curious, but then, as they started asking questions, they moved closer and became absorbed in my work in progress.

Their fascination only spurred me on. I loved the idea that these men, who on the surface didn't appear to be typical art gallery patrons, were so captivated by the painting process. Before long, we were bantering back and forth as I dabbed the paint on the canvas.

"Do you live around here?" I asked as I filled in the forms of the buildings.

"My mom lives in the next town," said Brad, the younger of the two. "We're just visiting."

"What kind of paintings do you like?" I asked, stopping to look at them directly.

"Landscapes," said Steve. "Street scenes," replied his buddy, Brad.

By now they had piqued my interest, and I couldn't resist asking the next question.

"Do you have a favorite painter?"

"Thomas Kinkade," they said, almost in unison.

My eyes must have twinkled, especially when another onlooker—a neighbor of mine—immediately broke the news about who I was.

At first Steve and Brad were in disbelief, but then they settled into an easy camaraderie and started telling me about themselves and what attracted them to my work. As it turned out, they were such big fans that only the day before, they had visited one of my galleries in a nearby mall. Steve, the owner of a contracting business, confessed that he regularly dragged his dates to my galleries to impress them—whether they wanted to go or not.

On the other hand, Brad, a handsome thirty-two-year-old, admitted he had sworn off dating until the right girl came along. He liked to drop into my galleries by himself, he said, because he found my paintings "happy, colorful, and uplifting." He explained that deep within each canvas, he found the sense of family, love, and stability he is yearning for—an affirmation that "it's possible to have a happy home life."

As I heard these two men share their innermost thoughts with me, a perfect stranger, I was humbled by their candor. We were strangers, and yet, through my paintings, through the creative outlet that God had put in my hands, we were connected. We could communicate about the things that mattered and for a brief time, at least, contribute something meaningful to one another's lives.

"This is like a God thing," said Brad. "We just stopped by for a cup of coffee—and we got to see Thomas Kinkade painting a picture of town!"

For me, their appearance was a "God thing," too. I found myself energized by their enthusiasm and filled with a renewed sense of purpose. Also, they gave me a gift needed by every person who aspires to creativity—an affirmation that what we are doing has some worth. This may seem a little disingenuous, coming from a person who makes a living as a painter and is frequently the focal point of various accolades. But no matter how many paintings or books we may sell—or how many good ideas we contribute to our particular corporation, or how much time or money we bestow on some worthy, not-for-profit cause—we still need positive, personal feedback from other human beings.

So I was consciously thankful for the God-given serendipity that had unexpectedly enriched this particular plein air experience. For an hour or so, Steve and Brad stood back watching as my painting progressed. By the time they left, it was ten-thirty in the morning and the painting was well under way, with all the masses blocked in and the forms of the scene beginning to emerge in recognizable contours.

The unplanned presence of these two young men had provided me with a tremendous surge of energy and creativity as I filled in the "payoff details," the fine strokes of color that would bring the painting alive. Almost without effort, I watched the shapes emerge: the chrome fender of the old car just in front of me; the light hitting the hills in the background; the sign on the nearby restaurant window, and the bricks on the pavement at my feet. Then I switched to my soft, fine sable-hair brush, dabbed it in the blob of burnt sienna on my palette, and started outlining the fine details of tree limbs and patches of dappled light.

These details were the pièces de résistance, the subtle touches that would help the painting "pop" off the canvas and shimmer like a jewel. But even though this particular workday was still unfolding, I knew at the end of the day, I would be satisfied. My cup of creativity had already been filled to overflowing by serendipity.

City by the Bay

THE LIGHT OF FREEDOM

A Quiet Patriot

ometimes, a great disaster—indeed, a national or global catastrophe—may trigger the creative impulse. That's what happened to me on that fateful day in September 2001.

Immediately after the tragedy of 9/11, I sat down in front of my easel and painted my response. The result was *The Light of Freedom,* which depicts a view of the Manhattan skyline from the south, with the Statue of Liberty holding a spark of light in the distance on the left and a cavity of huddled lights in the center where the Twin Towers once stood.

But the painting is dominated by an American flag, illuminated by a celestial light bursting through clouds high in the sky. The red-white-and-blue banner wafts from an eagle-crowned flagpole, which anchors and balances the right side of the painting, much as the Statue of Liberty solidly supports the left. But the dominant visual message is light—both a natural light that physically warms the flesh and the earth, and the Light of the World, who cuts through the darkness of evil and death.

When I painted this scene, I wanted to make a personal statement, or more accurately, issue an anguished cry about the changes these events had wrought in me and in the America I had come to know. Like everyone else, I didn't know what the future might hold. I still don't. I only knew that my spirit had been wounded deeply by this attack.

But even as I was hurting, I somehow also knew I was by no means down and out—and I wanted to get that point across. How did I feel? Upset, of course. Angry. Full of grief. But at the same time, I sensed a new resolve as a member of this special American society and culture. A fresh surge of creativity, symbolized by a different kind of light, was now moving me to try to think and feel and understand my life and my country on more profound levels.

After I finished *The Light of Freedom* and the painting had been shipped off for prints to be made, I wondered what I had really achieved in my studio. I questioned whether my creative efforts would remain largely personal, or whether they might touch some of the same emotional and patriotic chords in others that the creative act of painting had evoked in me.

The answer seems to be that many others responded to 9/11 much as I did: They have harbored the same feelings of devastation and grief—but also held on to the same hopes for the future. I believe that's why this painting has become one of my most popular.

But I hold on more tightly to special stories that drift in to me from around the country—such as the financial services executive who was actually working in a company branch on the fortieth floor of a midtown building when the disaster struck downtown. This executive, whom I'll call Jane, was on her way out of the office to a meeting across the street from the World Trade Center, but of course, circumstances changed all that.

"I wound up being one of the senior people in charge of making a lot of unexpected decisions," she recalled. "We didn't know whether this was an isolated incident or a general attack on the city."

And there were so many other considerations, apart from the unique business pressures. Jane's brother-in-law, for example, usually worked on a high floor of Tower Two, but that day he had missed his train. He was one of the few in his offices who survived.

Nine months after 9/11, Jane walked into a gallery to look for a picture for her sister's birthday. She stopped short when she saw on a wall in front of her a print of *The Light of Freedom*.

"It was overwhelming in the sense that it immortalized my experience," Jane said. "For me, the flag is such a symbol of freedom. But what I saw on that wall wasn't just a picture of the tragedy of the skyline. Rather, I was looking at the tenacity and commitment of the American people to rise above dire circumstances."

Jane bought two copies of the painting to leave each of her sons as a legacy. One now hangs as the centerpiece of the library in her home—in fact, she designed the library around the painting. "When people walk into the room, it's the first thing they see, hanging there over the fireplace."

It's impossible for me to describe how I feel when I hear stories like this. Memories of 9/11 still trigger deep emotions in me, and when I look at that particular painting, I revisit the pain of the tragedy I witnessed on television, as did most other Americans that fateful morning, and also the cathartic release I felt as I painted and completed that particular scene.

Sometimes, when you're thinking about your connection to a vast population, a nation, it's hard to feel patriotic. Yet when the connection to your nation becomes highly personal—as happened with the 9/11 attacks, or with the responses of people like Jane—patriotism can become one of the most powerful of emotions.

It was remarkable but completely understandable to me to watch everyone in our vast land—Californians, Texans, Minnesotans, Floridians—join in one voice to embrace the beleaguered New Yorkers. In a very real sense, we all experienced a close-to-home expression of community solidarity, reminiscent of John F. Kennedy's words of unity with "Berliners" when he visited West Berlin and the old Berlin Wall: *"Ich bin ein Berliner."*

Yes, after 9/11, I could say with considerable feeling, "I am a New Yorker." And I am also a new kind of American—a patriot with a new depth and intensity of commitment. But this patriotism isn't jingoistic or isolationist or unduly fearful. Rather, I'm gripped by a quiet loyalty and gratitude—an unabashed thankfulness that I'm part of a great community with personal roots buried deep in my country's soil. The reality of these events has made me more acutely conscious that we really have realized Rousseau's philosophical dream—that all people are "born free" even though most don't experience that birthright of freedom.

Yet my family and I are not only "born free"—we are *free in fact* because we live and work and thrive in this land. We are free to communicate, to believe, and to create as we see fit. Certainly, that's a weighty responsibility for all Americans—and especially for those of us who feel called to exercise and express our creative impulses.

In this century, perhaps more than any other, creativity is our birthright. And perhaps our success as a nation, when you boil it down, can be traced to the fact that creativity is also one of America's most valuable national resources.

THE FIFTH DAY
OF CREATIVE LIVING

The Joy of Work

Work thou for pleasure—paint, or sing, or carve
The thing thou lovest, though the body starve—
Who works for glory misses oft the goal;
Who works for money coins his very soul.
Work for the work's sake, then, and it may be
That these things shall be added unto thee.

—— FROM WORK, 1895, BY KENYON COX,
AMERICAN PAINTER AND CRITIC

ABUNDANT HARVEST

The Rhythm of Work

Creativity may be spawned through solitude, passion, love relationships, or community involvement. But in the end, to *get the job done,* you have to sit down at a desk, or position yourself in front of an easel, or take some other action. To put it bluntly, creativity will never happen without hard work.

On the other hand, work doesn't necessarily have to *be* work. If you can find your natural creative rhythm, you'll move into your project with maximum energy, enthusiasm, and staying power. Although rhythms may vary from person to person, many highly creative people have found several common threads in their experiences. Specifically, to use a metaphor from nature, creative rhythm will typically involve gestation, birth, and accelerating growth.

The beginning phase is characterized by a slow-moving, fallow period when nothing much seems to be happening. At this stage the individual does preliminary research and thinking in an effort to find the best insight, idea, or approach to take in expressing a deeply held passion. Then, when the idea or strategy is fully formed, a creative burst—or birth, if you will—breaks out into the open. Finally, as the person builds on the basic idea or insight, the final product takes shape with increasing rapidity until, at the end of the process, there may be a sense of flying through to the conclusion.

To get an idea of how this creative rhythm may play out in practice, consider another one of my recent plein air projects. I had spent considerable time in the gestation phase, thinking about how to execute the painting, which was to involve a particular mountain scene. I was certain that the light of late afternoon would be best, but something just wasn't clicking. As the project percolated in my mind, days and weeks went by, but still, I didn't schedule a time to go up the mountain road and start painting. In the back of my mind, something remained unresolved. So I waited . . . and waited.

After ruminating and meditating one particular day, a thought popped into my mind: *You've been considering this scene only as a sunset view. But I wonder—what would the treetopped ridge look like in the light of early morning?*

So just after dawn, I raced up the winding road on my motorbike, and this time, as I saw the emerging sunlight flickering on the distant peaks, I knew I had reached my moment of completion. The creative struggle—those nagging little questions that had engaged my mind for weeks—suddenly found release in the scene spread out before me. The light spilled across the valley, the long shadows of the redwoods reached like fingers into the road, the sunlight danced delicately through the trees, casting lacy shadows on the meadow, and the distant eucalyptus trees shimmered and glowed.

This is it! I thought to myself. *The hills awash in early morning light!* As the adrenaline surged through my veins, my mind began spinning with possibilities. Almost immediately, I moved into the third phase of creative rhythm—the growth of the idea, which accelerated at a faster and faster rate of speed.

Now, I knew exactly how I would balance the large forms, move one prominent crest off-center, introduce dramatic long shadows, and entice the viewer's eye back into deep space through the recurrent vertical lines of the receding lines of trees. I knew, too, how I would render the distant mountains in that hazy blue tone of morning. And I understood how I would create a warm undertone to the sky as it rose gradually to the bowl of the heavens.

The ideal proportion of the canvas even dawned on me: a five-by-six format, which is the squarest in my repertoire. The view screamed out for a square composition that would allow the verticals to breathe and give me enough dimensionality to place bushes and other elements in the extreme foreground, yet still carry the viewer's eye back deep into the painting.

My vision that morning—the creative birth after a long period of gestation—was a revelation, almost a Damascus road experience that blinded me with its intensity. It may seem sacrilegious to liken a painter's epiphany to the Apostle Paul's divine encounter on the Damascus road, but the light of inspiration seems like that at times. It is indeed blinding and overwhelming, a torrent of insight that can break through the ordinary anytime, anywhere, to put us in touch with the creative mind of the Master Artist.

The ancient Scriptures tell us that without a vision people perish, and nowhere is that more true than in our daily lives. Without a vision for our work, our family, or our relationships, we lose our broader focus on the basic meaning of life.

Yet this vision—containing the main idea that best expresses our greatest passion—is almost always borne of a creative rhythm, which includes a significant period of waiting. If we *expect* this initial time of waiting or gestation during the creative process, we will be much more likely to recognize the great vision when it arrives—and better prepared to transform that vision into a significant work of imagination.

COBBLESTONE MILL

Fashioning Your Flow

Although the initial phase of the creative rhythm may at first seem to be passive or immobile, this period of gestation and waiting actually presents us with a paradox. What may initially seem to be static or inert actually encompasses a turbulent flow of ideas and insights, always moving, ever traveling toward an unseen destination.

Like a mountain stream, the inner rivulets may meander gently or even go underground for a time. But then the current typically breaks through to the surface and proceeds to rush in torrents of ideas, conversations, and work preparations, crashing around and through obstacles and cascading over cliffs in a burst of power and energy. The flow may grow quiet once again as it courses along—and the creative project unfolds—but always, relentlessly, the inner imaginative impulse moves forward.

Yet many may wonder, "This all sounds fine in the abstract, but let's assume I've come up with a great idea. How can I jump-start my creative engines and get started?"

Here are some suggestions for initiating your personal roller-coaster ride through the hills and valleys of the creative process:

Prepare in Advance

The best insurance policy for a creative day is to plan your activity in advance—and in as much detail as possible. With this prior preparation, you'll be in a much stronger position to take full advantage of each moment of inspiration when it hits you.

You might be planning a birthday party for your eight-year-old, rolling out an ad campaign, or getting ready to compose a symphony. Whatever your objective, it's important to do the advance legwork. Think through the details, do any necessary research, and have your equipment ready. That way, when your "creative appointment" is finally upon you, you'll be able to focus on riding the creative flow of that particular day, without being concerned about minutiae.

Take a cue from my friend Priscilla, who gave a speech recently at a church women's luncheon. As part of her presentation, she was planning to screen a short video clip with a powerful inspirational message. In addition, she came up with the idea to have several friends on hand to be available afterward to pray with anyone who had an unusual burden.

The week before her speech, Priscilla practiced aloud every day so that she would be free to make constant eye contact with her audience. She even invited her friends over to her house to view the video clip and pray in advance for the women at the luncheon.

To make sure that she wouldn't overlook any of her audience's needs, she printed up special cards for people to write down prayer requests and purchased a supply of pens. Finally, she found some bright red shopping bags that could identify her friends and serve as a collection spot for the prayer cards.

On the day of the event, Priscilla arrived early, cued up the tape and checked the VCR, and explained to her friends when to pass out cards and pens and where to position themselves for prayer after the luncheon.

The speech came off like clockwork. But even more important, because of the extensive preparation, Priscilla and her friends were able to avoid mistakes related to poor planning during the luncheon and thus could make themselves totally available to the women in the audience. They were ready, for example, when a woman approached and confided a deep concern that she hadn't yet shared with anyone else: Her son, who was an agricultural specialist in the Philippines, was missing. Fearing the worst, the woman asked for help. The prayer team immediately lifted up the man in prayer—and the next day, miraculously, he called home to report that he was alive and well.

Block Out a Specific Work Time and Expect to Be Creative

One independent public relations rep I know often devotes his mornings to family responsibilities, and so by the time the afternoon comes around, his mind is still racing with "to-do" lists. But he's developed a surefire method for clearing out the mental clutter and getting ready to write or interact with clients: he takes a half-hour catnap in his office. When he wakes up, his mind is clear and he is able to forge ahead with confidence that the ideas will eventually flow. And for him, they always do—but only after that nap!

Surround Yourself with Creative People

Although I'm an artist, I don't tend to socialize with other artists because I find the conversations often too predictable. Instead, I fill my evenings and weekends with friendships cut from a different creative cloth—business entrepreneurs, filmmakers, and actors. One of my favorite people made a fortune in business and retired early to manage his investments and devote himself to his passion for birds. Now all he does is build birdcages nonstop. He builds them and hand-paints them and gives them away to friends. He works with his kids, plays golf, and builds birdcages. How can you not want to be around a guy who builds birdcages all day long?

Some weekends, what we do for fun is go out to dinner with our wives at neighborhood roadhouses—especially those with overly loud local bands. After dinner we'll dance and then play a few rounds of gin rummy for a nickel a point—which no one ever seems to pay! The creative synergy of four people playing games and dancing is incredible—and for the price of a cheap dinner I get my mental engines revved up and I'm ready to attack my work the very next day.

Take One Small Step

How many times have you said to yourself, "I'd like to write, but I'm waiting for inspiration"? To my way of thinking, that's a contradiction in terms. Inspiration is all around and above and inside you. You don't have to wait for it to appear magically—just open your eyes! The same is true of every deep question or challenge you may be facing in your life. The way to find the answer isn't by sitting around and fretting. The answers come by trial and error.

As an illustration, consider the way the design for my galleries developed. My business had begun to grow, and I had the sense I should expand into galleries, but I wasn't sure what interior would be the most appealing. Should the galleries be white and hard-edged, like most contemporary art spaces, or should they be designed in some radical new way?

In the back of my mind, I had an offbeat idea to turn the tables on the usual gallery experience and make the Kinkade galleries warm and homey. I envisioned hunter-green walls, fireplaces, and comfy chairs. I pictured a mood-filled atmosphere, where the lighting shone primarily on the paintings, making them focal points of light and inspiration against the subtle walls. And I imagined friendly staff members, who weren't necessarily art "experts," but rather were everyday people who loved sharing the joy of art with others.

Instead of agonizing over the details, or holding back on the idea until the optimum moment came along, I took a bold step. In 1991, I opened my first gallery designed exactly as I had envisioned it.

By God's grace, our first humble effort succeeded. Within ten years, we repeated our success in gallery after gallery all over the world, until now we can honestly feel proud to have created the largest chain of art galleries on the planet.

Your creative field may be quite different from mine. Maybe you want to become an accomplished pianist or violinist. Or perhaps you'd like to be known as the "idea person" on your favorite community or church committee. But regardless of your particular area of creative interest, you and I face many of the same basic problems—and the first is that we must move from idea to execution, from imagination to practical application. So what are you waiting for? Go ahead—take that first step.

Cobblestone Mill

STEPPING STONE COTTAGE

When Paintings Speak

Too often, those aspiring to greater creative productivity feel stymied, distracted, or even a little bored as they walk into the office or workspace to face the day's demands. I know most of the typical responses and feelings—because at one time or another, I've felt them myself:

- "I'd really rather be out in the sunshine than here in this studio."
- "What about those bills and phone calls? I think my work can wait."
- "I can always get started later this morning or this afternoon."
- "I'm really tired after that party last night. Maybe tomorrow . . ."

One way to overcome such obstacles is to find a new way to approach your work so that it beckons and entices you into the creative flow. You might begin by recognizing the temptation that confronts us all to view work projects in a totally detached fashion—in effect as inanimate tasks that lie "out there," passively waiting to be shaped by human imagination.

Instead, I'd suggest that you turn this attitude upside down. Try using your imagination to transform your work, or some aspect of it, into a personal "friend" or "companion" or "collaborator." Then, try interacting with your work product much as you would with another person. Ask questions, express your deepest feelings—indeed, *speak* to your work. If you do, you may be surprised to find that you are starting to look forward to launching each day's work.

How might this personalizing of your work play out in practice?

Again, let me explain with a personal illustration. In my studio, where I do most of my work, a painting may grow and develop over weeks, months, and sometimes even years as I modify, embellish, or perfect a work in progress. Eventually, each painting takes on a distinct personality, which matures and blossoms until the final brushstroke finishes the job. So every morning when I enter my studio and prepare to continue my work of the previous day, I greet a "friend" on the easel who is both an extension of my personality and aspirations, and also an individual entity with unique character traits.

Also, I never work on just one painting at a time. Instead, like friends and colleagues whom I've invited to a wonderful party, fifty or more canvases in various states of completion perch on racks running all around my studio.

Throughout the day, as my eye wanders around the room scanning the racks, these paintings in a sense actually "speak" to me, sometimes individually and sometimes in a group chorus. Sometimes, this silent communication is as gentle as a whisper. Sometimes, a work in progress actually seems to be crying out to me.

Typically, I'll "sense" these communications wafting out at different tempos and decibel levels when I stop for a drink of water or take a break for a phone call. One might whisper to me, saying, "I need some more detailing, though I'm not quite sure where." Another might speak more plainly: "Come over here. I need some attention with these colors." Still another might shout, "I need a new composition, *now*!"

The minute I hear a painting "speak," I immediately drop what I'm doing—even if I'm in the middle of an important phone call—and respond.

"Excuse me—but I have to do something," I said the other day to one business colleague who was patiently trying to make a point from the other end of the phone.

Hearing a whisper from one of my paintings, I put down the phone, ran over to the painting, and sketched in a little reminder of the painting's "message" in chalk right on top of the near-finished canvas. On other occasions, perhaps I'll jot down an idea on a Post-it Note and stick it on the surface of a painting.

Sometimes a painting is nearly finished when I sense—or am "notified" by the work itself—that something is amiss. My eye might land on a figure whose leg looks wrong, for example, and I'll put a big arrow next to the limb as a reminder to rework it. If the painting speaks loudly enough, I might even throw it up on my easel, grab a two-inch housepainter's brush, and start reworking—often with an entirely new direction in mind.

One painting sat in my studio for seven years without so much as a peep. I let it sit dormant until it finally "announced" that it was ready. Within a few days the painting was finished, and soon it became a successful print release. Just imagine: a finished work in exactly seven years— plus a few days! But it is those final few days of feverish inspiration that count most.

A Peaceful Time

Basket-Weaving

When we hear the word *creativity,* the first description that comes to mind may be "burst of inspiration," or "brilliant imagination," or "profound insight." In fact, the most common component of creativity is much more down-to-earth or even mundane. Certainly, the creative experience will often begin with a fresh idea or insight. But the realization and execution of that idea—which is an essential part of any creative process—is most likely to involve what I call *basket-weaving,* or the plodding exercise of hard-won skills through diligent effort.

The creation of an actual high-quality basket begins with the acquisition of intricate physical weaving skills, plus some fresh idea about how to apply those skills. But this is only the beginning. To bring the idea and skills to fruition, it's necessary to engage in the repetitive, sometimes tedious act of weaving the final product. Without this final phase, the skills and ideas mean nothing.

If you reflect for a moment, you can probably come up with many examples of the basket-weaving phase of creativity:

> A tennis player may devise an imaginative strategy to beat
> a difficult opponent. But she knows she'll have to work
> out the kinks in long hours of practice and then spend
> much of the game working the other player around the
> court—tennis basket-weaving, if you will—until she can
> finally set up just the right situation for her brilliant finishing shot.

⟶ A gardener sitting in the quiet of his study conceives of a beautiful configuration of flowers. But then he must plant the seeds and cultivate the shoots over weeks or months for the original vision to be realized.

⟶ The adviser or mentor tutoring a teenager often must spend hours building confidence or teaching basic skills—until finally, the confidence and lessons "click" and the student excels on an exam or independent project.

Interestingly, even though such basket-weaving may sometimes seem repetitious or mindless, these periods of building methodically toward a climax often spark further creative insights, sometimes even more significant than the original vision. In his book *The Breakout Principle,* Dr. Herbert Benson of Harvard Medical School actually identifies biochemical changes that occur in the mind and body during familiar, repetitive tasks. Many times, he says, these changes are associated with enhanced creativity—and I can certainly concur with this analysis.

So when you're doing something routine before, during, or after a major act of creation—such as stuffing envelopes for a political campaign after you've conceptualized a surefire strategy for winning an election—don't be repelled by the monotony. Instead, expect exciting breakouts of creativity in completely unrelated areas.

I've experienced some of my most creative moments while I'm in the basket-weaving stage of the artistic cycle—that more mechanical, busy-work phase that's required after initial bursts of creativity. Whenever I hit the basket-weaving phase, the motion of my hand becomes pure intuition. An hour into painting a recent landscape, years of experience kicked in as I massed up blobs of paint and pulled out forms to create the image impressed on my visual memory. With my inner eye, I could see exactly where I was going on the canvas, and my hand became a mere extension of my vision, rather than something I needed to direct at will.

During such experiences the creative enterprise—whether in art, science, or business—enters a remote-control stage in which the mind is free to engage in other kinds of creative acts. I suppose this is what others have called "multitasking," or "multiphasic thinking." In other words, as I proceed with the basket-weaving stage of a painting, I can easily take a phone call from a reporter or work out a business deal with one of my associates—without missing a beat. Or I may listen to books on tape, an idea I picked up from Norman Rockwell, who arranged to have books read to him by his models as he worked.

Music also helps keep my creative juices flowing during the basket-weaving phase, especially Bach's *Brandenburg Concertos,* which have always struck me as musical puzzles that the mind could gnaw on endlessly with ever-increasing satisfaction. I could listen to such works over and over, and I frequently do. Here I take my cue from Leonardo da Vinci, who reportedly painted the *Mona Lisa* while listening to music played by a chamber orchestra he invited to his studio.

Breakthroughs during basket-weaving have been replicated time and again in many other settings. More often than I can remember, a transforming creative impulse has emerged during the basket-weaving phase of my painting. So you can see why I often look with great anticipation beyond the intense bursts of imagination to seek insights in quieter stretches of artistic craftsmanship.

TEACUP COTTAGE

Funny Business

Periodic breaks are essential to achieve maximum creativity, and I've found no better way to take a break than to inject some humor into the mix. Many scientific studies and patient reports have suggested that regular fun fests, joke sessions, and belly laughs not only are helpful in generating fresh ideas, but may also benefit one's health and well-being.

Humor has been my tonic ever since I was young. My circle of buddies and I—along with friends who might be visiting—used to get a great kick out of turning art into games during those early grade school years. I still recall the great pleasure we got out of drawing airplanes, ships, and tanks, which we then injected into war scenes with appropriate childish sound effects:

"Zoom! Swoosh! Screech! Boom!" A direct hit on an enemy vehicle could mean a frantic scribbling of obliterating lines—and often a torn page!

The dramatic, emotional sound effects brought the art to life and, the next time around, always motivated me to improve on my previous creative performance.

Bigger opportunities for playing around artistically came in my early twenties, when I hooked up with my art-school friend Jim Gurney for that cross-country rail-riding escapade I mentioned earlier. Jim was later the best man in my wedding and the author of the book *Dinotopia*.

But at the time, our plan was to take our sketchbooks and discover America. We hoped to have some adventures and rub shoulders with real people who could teach us things we had been missing in the artificial environment of art school. To make a few extra dollars, we fashioned ourselves as "sketch artists" and determined to draw portraits of people along the way.

We had our routine down pat. With some preprinted signs that said "Portrait Sketches, Done While-U-Wait" in hand, we marched into a tavern or coffee shop at each stop on our route and announced, "We will draw anyone for $2 a throw!"

Before long, we were rolling in money—or at least enough to buy a meal and get us to the next town. Guys were particularly eager to have us sketch their girlfriends, but early on, we learned that you can't draw girls too accurately. If you draw them the way they actually appear, with the imperfections in complexion or the idiosyncrasies of facial features, women won't like it. Men on the other hand, will let you push their portraits to the limit, almost to the point of caricature. Typically, a girl would take one look at our sketch, turn to her boyfriend, and complain, "That doesn't look a thing like me!"

"I'm not paying," the boyfriend would have to say, to hold up his protective image.

After one or two of these fiascoes, we quickly got creative and simply portrayed our female subjects as stereotyped, Barbie-esque forms with a big-eyed, perfect-featured face, to which we added the right hair color and hairdo for the girl we were sketching. The girl smiled, her boyfriend got a kiss, and we pocketed the two bucks. All the way to the next town, we chuckled at the all-too-common foibles of human vanity.

Perhaps the biggest—and most needed—belly laughs in my career erupted back in California at Ralph Bakshi Studios, after Jim and I landed jobs as the "background team" for the 1983 movie *Fire and Ice*. In those days, before the advent of computer animation, that meant we had to paint the backgrounds against which the characters would move. I guess we did about thirteen hundred or so paintings for this project—fanciful, imaginative worlds that might require a jungle, ice kingdom, or whatever.

The two of us were doing the work of what would usually involve a background team of ten or more people, and so we had to hustle to get the job done. The pressure mounted when it became clear that the whole movie schedule depended heavily on our meeting tough deadlines. Although we were getting paid very well for twenty-two-year-olds and we loved the work, we still needed to relieve the pressure. Humor was our natural outlet to keep the creative intensity at a high pitch.

One ploy we used might be called the "pudding-paint prank." Jim is right-handed and I am left-handed, and so we typically placed the paint containers in a space between us so that we both would have access. But in the midst of the real paint jars, we'd place a little jar filled with chocolate pudding. Then, when strangers came into the room, we'd launch into our scenario.

One day, the producers brought some Japanese investors and other movie bigwigs into our room. We didn't look up, but when they were all gathered around, ready to watch how the creative process worked, I said, "I need a little more burnt umber over here."

I then dipped a clean paintbrush into the chocolate pudding, and before painting a stroke, I licked the "paint" into my mouth. After I had sampled the brown goo, I looked at Jim and asked, "How old is that paint? It tastes pretty bad."

Jim tasted a sample. "This paint is spoiled!" he shouted.

"Good thing we didn't paint with it," I repled nonchalantly.

The response from the investors was a predictable "Ooooo," and I've often wondered what went through their minds. Maybe they really did think something especially creative was going on between us. Or maybe they just thought we were nuts.

All I know is that after this kind of bantering and practical joking, Jim and I always felt invigorated and enthused—and better prepared to create as we entered our fanciful world once again.

You may not want to go this far in devising practical jokes to rejuvenate your creative rhythms, and you don't have to. Instead, just go out with some crazy, fun friends for an evening, or play a simpleminded parlor game at home, or clown around in the pool with the kids. Or learn by heart a routine from your favorite comedian and present it at your next gathering of friends or church talent show. I do all these things—both because they relieve the creative intensity of my typical workday, and also just because they're fun.

In the last analysis, though, humor is a big key to my own creativity because I often find that during these light and hilarious moments, I see my work in entirely new ways. New insights and ideas pop into my head. And filled to the brim with enthusiasm and great expectations, I'm ready once more to return to the easel.

HOME IS WHERE THE HEART IS II

The Mathematics of Creativity

The creative rhythms of work encompass not just nonrational bursts of insight and imagination, but also profound intellectual effort. In other words, you can't leave your mind and your rational faculties at the door when you embark on a creative quest. As a creative person, you need not only the big, earthshaking ideas, but also the analytical skills and knowledge to enable you to *think through* hard problems that arise in daily work—and to reason your way to the right solution.

In fact, I believe this rational component in creativity is fundamental to the way we and the rest of nature have been constructed. To understand better how this works, travel with me in your imagination back to that very first act of creation—the one where God got everything started *ex nihilo*. I've already referred to that original seven-day event as the work of a Master Artist, but actually that's only part of the story. In fact, God was at least as much a mathematician as an artist, as he fashioned and shaped our world and all that's in it.

The fundamental principle we must recognize—and learn to use—is that a rational structure lies behind all reality and applies to whatever creative endeavor we are pursuing. This includes *any* of our interests, whether an accounting problem, a management conundrum, an environmental project, a child-rearing challenge—or any conceptual roadblock that impedes our progress with the traditional arts, such as poetry, prose, piano compositions, or painting. In most cases, you have to grasp the nuts and bolts underlying a creative act before you can achieve a finished product.

Part of the reason we need to understand the nuts and bolts of our particular reality is that everything—and I mean *everything*—in this world is constructed of small, complex parts. And the more we understand how to manipulate those parts, the more likely it is that we can become experts at producing something worthwhile on a grander scale.

When I'm musing on this topic as a painter, I tend to think in more scientific terms, probably because of my love of math. So my thinking may proceed like this:

When I'm painting a landscape, what I see in nature—and what I see emerging on the canvas—is only a small part of the reality that lies in front of me. On the purely inanimate level—inside the various solids and liquids and gases—the underlying atomic and molecular structure is nothing less than amazing. On an even tinier plane, theoretical physicists and mathematicians hypothesize that the landscape becomes even more complex and turbulent, with quantum foam, extra-dimensional strings, and subatomic particles galore.

But then I move up to the "macro" level, to various life-forms—from complex vegetation to increasingly intelligent animals and, finally, to the pinnacle of creation, the self-conscious human being. At these upper levels of reality, the underlying mathematical complexity becomes breathtaking and often incomprehensible to me. Imagine trying to explain—or portray on a painter's canvas—the interplay of our twenty-three pairs of human chromosomes, our thirty thousand–plus genes, and our trillions of cells—not to mention the activity of our DNA, RNA, amino acids, and enzymes.

The sheer number of tiny components that underlie our natural or artistically created world is a staggering thought. And when I consider that these components also constantly interact in countless combinations with one another, the mathematical implications transport me into a realm of theory and calculation that's well beyond my comprehension.

For many people who hope to improve their creative expression, a contemplation of such factual detail and intricacy may be not only *not* inspiring, but downright dismaying. I can hear the protests well up on several levels:

— "I wasn't aware that Manet or Steinbeck or Mozart was a rocket scientist or a math whiz."

— "Are you saying I need multiple graduate degrees—or a library with thousands of arcane books—before I can draw a flower or write a poem?"

— "If I have to become an expert in far-flung fields, how can I expect to make any headway when I'm trying to come up with a creative solution to a personnel issue at work?"

Well, even though I paint landscapes, I'm certainly not an expert geologist or botanist or mathematician, and I don't have any graduate degrees in such fields. Furthermore, nobody ever calls on me to exhibit any special skills or knowledge in those areas.

But I've done my best over the years, mainly through research, strategic reading, and self-teaching, to absorb the crucial information I need to do my absolutely best job as a painter. Similarly, I believe it's up to all who want to maximize their creativity to exercise and expand their minds, not only in their special chosen field but in related fields as well. Unless we continue to develop new intellectual skills—and are stimulated through exposure to other disciplines—our creative impulses will never mature.

Let me demonstrate with a few illustrations from the realm I know best, my own experience as a painter. To begin with, I believe the *most* creative phase of my painting involves math, especially decisions I must make about geometric proportions and shapes. Specifically, I have found that if I hope to succeed, I must begin each of my works with blocking-out processes I call "underdrawing" and "massing."

First, I use pencil or charcoal to sketch in some of the main elements or figures that will dominate the painting. Then I apply an undertone color, such as blue or brown, in different amounts and hues to indicate how I plan to shift the overall "weight" of the work in one direction or another on the canvas.

A tremendous amount of thought and imagination goes into this early phase of the creative process, in part because these initial decisions will determine the basic balance or "equilibrium" of the final work. After I've completed the underdrawing and massing, I am able to fix permanently in my mind—in a kind of vision painted indelibly on my imagination—the details of the various proportions, shapes, and relationships that will emerge in the finished picture.

I often say that for me, this early massing and weighting has to be absolutely drum-tight with no loose ends or major uncertainties. In other words, I have to be able to picture in my mind's eye at this early phase *precisely* what will emerge on the blank canvas. I have to know beyond any question that a particular stream will flow here, a mountain will rise there, or a house or gazebo will occupy another spot. The painting becomes a kind of map or mathematical equation in which all the pieces have to be correctly ordered.

Believe it or not, this early stage of composition—which could go on for hours, days, or even weeks—is the most intense part of the creative process. For me, conceptualization, spatial composition, and massing require the utmost concentration and hard work to be certain that I know precisely where everything will be situated, how the colors and tonal values will mesh, and how every part of the picture will relate to every other part. If I succeed at this stage, the painting will fall into place easily and naturally over the successive process of execution. But if I fall short in this initial conceptualization, I can expect that extra challenges will lie ahead. As with master chess players whose opening moves will determine the outcome of the game, so the artist must lay the proper foundation for later success to occur.

An analogy to all this can be found in the field of professional writing. Many writers will say that if they can just settle on an "angle," or basic theme, for a book or article and then come up with a good organization for their presentation, they're more than halfway home to a finished product.

After this preliminary conceptualization, they are free to let their creative impulses roam freely within the fixed outline. In other words, they can proceed with the "basket-weaving" that we discussed earlier. But if they fail to make smart, specific decisions at the outset about their precise theme and organization, they'll pay a big price later in terms of a confused and inferior piece of work.

This early, analytical part of the creative process of painting reminds me of how, as a young mathematics student, I often approached a difficult math problem. Before I ever put pencil to paper, I might spend long minutes or even hours in creative analysis—thinking, imagining, and dreaming about ways to solve the problem. But when I finally saw the right approach—the exact formula or equation that would lead to the solution—all that remained was to plug in the numbers and do the calculations.

Again, the creative process in conceptualizing and constructing a painting is much the same. An inkling of these mathematical foundations of creativity crept into my consciousness while I was an art student at the Art Center College of Design in Pasadena, California. During a class on perspective drawing, my teacher, Ted Youngkin, followed a philosophy that if you created a deep need in a student, that student might spend the rest of his life trying to fill it. For me, he created a deep hunger for mathematical precision and taught me techniques that could be used to satisfy that hunger. I've used those and other mathematical techniques ever since in designing and creating my paintings.

Ted would propose hypothetical situations and then give us the mental tools to solve the problem. He would say, for example, "Suppose you wanted to draw some brick garden steps leading up to a flat platform. At the base of the steps is a puddle, which is reflecting the stairway. How would you draw the steps, including the lines of the brick, in perspective and then calculate the perspective of the stairway reflected in the puddle?"

Now this may sound a little arcane or geeky to some people, but to me, it felt as though someone had lit a rocket under my brain and my mind was blasting off to the moon. I had been a bit of a math whiz in high school, but I had never considered the degree to which mathematics could apply to my art. To me, that was an astonishing insight that opened the door to a creative world far more expansive than anything I had ever imagined.

On another occasion, Ted posed this hypothetical: "Suppose you want to draw a striped lighthouse up on a hill. How are you going to calculate and draw the tower's ellipses so that they gradually increase in degree the closer you get to the top of the lighthouse?"

I could hardly wait for him to stop talking so I could try to solve the problem he had posed. Through such mental stimulation, I gradually mastered the systems needed to analyze the real world, with its varied straight lines and curves and angles and surfaces, and to accurately reproduce that three-dimensional scene on a two-dimensional surface. In other words, I gradually learned the secrets of representational art. But this turned out to be an issue that couldn't be resolved during one art class or even after many hard nights of study and practice. Sure, I quickly learned how to draw a simple ellipse. But it took years for me to become adept at orchestrating multiple ellipses in a particular scene to suggest height or movement, or to draw the viewer more deeply into the painting itself.

As I have pursued my art, my respect has increased for the insights Ted Youngkin shared during that early art class. He not only stimulated me intellectually, he also introduced me to the powerful principle that a comprehensive rational structure—which can be understood only after the acquisition of significant knowledge and practical skills—underlies the creation of any beautiful, powerful work of art.

This structural foundation applies to all forms of creative expression—not just paintings, or poetry, or novels, or musical compositions, but every genuine act of creativity that you or anyone else may be pursuing. So now, you may want to explore the phase of your own personal development. To this end, ask yourself three questions:

1. "What additional skills seem important for me to do my creative work better?"
2. "What additional knowledge seems important for me to move to the next level in my creative quest?"
3. "When I compare myself with others in my field who have achieved mastery, what background or skills do they have that I lack—and what can I do to overcome that lack?"

Run these questions over in the back of your mind for a day or two, and you'll discover that an action plan is beginning to unfold—a plan that suggests special "formulas" and "equations" that comprise part of your own special mathematics of creativity.

Home Is Where the Heart Is II

CLOCKTOWER COTTAGE

Carpenter's Tools

To be successful, every creative effort requires practical tools. But whatever your field of interest, don't just jump willy-nilly into the creative process without first thinking through exactly what instruments you will need to express yourself effectively. Most experts in any field find that without the right tools, they can't expect to excel in their work.

When I say "tools," by the way, I mean all those physical instruments and aids that enable us to do creative work. In the broadest sense, this can include pens, pencils, paper, computers, software programs, paintbrushes, work surfaces, you name it. The list could run on and on for pages.

So how should you pick the creative tools that will help you achieve maximum creativity?

Probably the best first step is to check what other experts in your field are using and then, through practical application, test to see if their tools work for you. Don't worry if you find you feel more comfortable with tools that are different from those of the next guy. Above all, the tools you select should fit your particular personality and creative needs. In any event, the chances are that as you gain increasing expertise, your tools will evolve into instruments that fit you, but maybe no one else.

For example, one writer may select a computer with an advanced word-processing program, while another may prefer an old-fashioned typewriter.

Similarly, to be maximally creative in the pulpit, one preacher may require a particular well-worn Bible and typed notes. Another may speak from a complete script on a computer or teleprompter screen. And a third may not use notes at all and instead rely on extensive writing and outlining during preparation.

In the business world, one corporate chief executive may direct an assistant to prepare a summary of the day's news stories the first thing every morning. Another may prefer to do his own direct reading in several favorite newspapers.

In the world of art, the tools are as varied as the individual. One artist may prefer pastels while another goes for watercolors. Still another may choose traditional oils, with live models, floral arrangements, and other real subjects. As for me, my oil painting involves a rather peculiar if not unorthodox set of tools:

— My palette paper for mixing colors is an industrial-size roll of specially coated stock usually used in the meatpacking industry.

— For reference, I frequently rely on my large collection of miniaturized scale models of humans, animals, buildings, automobiles—even baby buggies, bicycles, and street lamps!

— My easel is a massive, custom-made contraption standing more than ten feet tall and featuring counterbalanced swing arms for constructing delicate perspective calculations. It looks more like something from a machine shop than from a studio.

— Many of my work tools are items commonly used by craftsmen, carpenters—even chemists and taxidermists.

In other words, I may be an oil painter, but you'd never know it from my tool chest or the shelves and closets in my studio. Sure, there are the usual paintbrushes and countless tubes of paint. But there's a constantly evolving assembly of improvised aids and devices—and the disconcerting variety points to an interesting link between creativity and tools. In fact, an often overlooked dimension of creativity involves the choice of tools.

Some aspiring artists, writers, or "idea people" in corporations give a low priority to choosing their tools of the trade. But if you're closed-minded or inflexible in your tool selection, it's likely that your finished painting, manuscript, or business proposal will lack a certain degree of verve and originality. Also, with an inadequate or limited tool selection, it's likely that it will take far too long to complete your finished product.

To see how my particular tools work to enhance my creativity and productivity, let's look at the above list in a little more detail. As you're reflecting on some of my strategies, you might ask yourself, "How can I select my tools so as to enhance my own creative flow?"

My Palette

Many artists still use the old-fashioned method of dabbing the colors they plan to use on a wooden or glass-topped palette. Then, when the surface gets messy or the artist needs a new set of colors, they have to interrupt their creative flow to clean and prepare it again.

I started out working that way, but I eventually found a much more efficient way to operate—an approach that contributes to my creativity because it minimizes the number of unnecessary interruptions. Years ago I improvised a palette table that features a bracket designed to hold a one-thousand-foot roll of coated industrial paper. Every day, I roll out an exposed two-foot section and begin mixing my paint on the paper as I would on a more traditional palette. After finishing with this section of palette paper, I simply scroll up the used portion, pull out two more feet of clean surface, and begin mixing my colors again. Voilà! I have a constantly fresh mixing area without ever having to clean a palette—an enormous savings in effort and mess.

As for my paints, instead of keeping the oils in tubes, I squeeze daubs of pigment into small plastic cups attached to a board. That way, every night I can store the board in my studio refrigerator to keep the oils fresh for the next day's work. For every painting, I prepare a separate board and store it on its own shelf in the refrigerator, a procedure that spares me from rummaging through piles of paint tubes to find the colors I need. If you were to peek into the refrigerator, you would see shelf after shelf of boards covered with paint-filled plastic cups—but I'm the only one who knows which shelf belongs to which painting.

My Reference

Early in my painting career, I learned that trying to find real people or objects to pose for me was too cumbersome—and not really necessary since I'm a landscape and scene painter, not a specialist in portraiture or still life. So I launched an effort to invent ways to find elements I needed from other sources.

Finally the answer came to me. Why not just assemble a wide collection of scale miniatures of the objects I needed so they would be ready for reference when needed in a given painting? So over the years, I have gradually filled an entire room with shelf after shelf of scale models, toys, figurines, collector's objects, dollhouse accessories, imported porcelain replicas—all of which portray, in miniature, the elements I frequently include as accents in my imaginary landscapes. If I need a grazing deer—I have one, beautifully rendered in cold-cast resin, ready to pose for my painting. A vintage milk truck? Third shelf up on the left is a timeless scale model, complete with rearview mirrors, hood ornament, and even miniaturized milk barrels.

I constantly browse antique shops, curio sellers, toy catalogs, and even conventions for collectors of porcelain figurines to find new treasures that can become props in future works. Frequently, the discovery of a new prop can even stimulate the creation of an unforeseen painting. I remember *Saturday Evening Post* illustrator Norman Rockwell describing an instance when he came upon an ornate vintage fireman's hat. He posed a friend in the imposing headpiece and soon had completed his memorable portrayal of an indignant aging fireman snubbing his nose at a smoldering cigar. It was a classic example of the serendipity of the creative process. In my case, the discovery at a woodsman's craft shop of a handmade birchbark canoe in miniature launched an entire series of paintings featuring canoes in wooded settings. You just never know how your tools will inspire creativity.

My Carpenter's Tools

In some respects, I think I'm as much a carpenter as I am an oil painter. It all begins with my choice of formats—an extremely important decision for any experienced artist. If you choose the wrong-size format, you're likely to run out of room at the top or on the sides—or you may have too much room. This kind of early misjudgment could make it impossible to achieve your ultimate goal.

With a particular painting I may choose dimensions such as two-by-three, three-by-four, or some other ratio. In every case, I'm guided by what I perceive as the demands of the scene I plan to paint.

As I proceed with my drafting and painting, a format challenge could necessitate resizing of the image. To achieve this, I scribe a new format onto the image using a sliding T-square device built into my easel and then carry the project into the wood shop. Using clamps, carpenter's straight-edges, and an electric skill saw, I cut the panel to the new dimensions, sand off any frayed canvas strands, and remount the work in progress on my easel.

My other carpenter's and draftsman's tools include Dremel® tools for cutting and scraping built-up paint residue, ellipse guides, and multiple measuring devices such as adjustable triangles, gravity-fed angle mea-surers, and chalk-coated snaplines. You name it, and I've probably got it.

I mention this array of tools simply to stimulate your thinking as you prepare to engage in your own creative work. The main message is this: Don't limit yourself to what others traditionally use in your field, or to what's worked well in the past, or to what others say you should use, or even to what you personally think you ought to use. "Shoulds" and "oughts" and outmoded traditions don't work well in any creative effort. Instead, begin to dream of ways that you might employ unusual or cutting-edge tools of technology—in addition to the simpler instruments that have served you well in the past. Why, just last week I was fascinated by my den-tist's new line of light-cured putty for use in dental fillings. Perhaps I will experiment with the stuff as a new means of creating texture on canvas. I wonder . . .

SIMPLER TIMES

The Power of Simplicity

The most powerful creative tools for anyone—architect, painter, writer, scientist, student, or businessperson—are a blank sheet of paper and a pencil.

These tools cost next to nothing, but they open worlds of rich possibilities within your imagination. That's why as an artist I'm so passionate about inspiring kids to draw with pencil and paper. In the simplicity of those materials lies the ultimate, unlimited form of creativity. There are no bounds to it. You could take that paper and render a detailed drawing of a building. Or you could take the paper and put a simple X on it. Or you could draw one circle or fifty interlocking circles. Or you could draw hideous monsters or sublimely beautiful maidens. There's no limit to creative expression.

What's more, such simple tools give you the chance to break out creatively anyplace, at any time—on an airplane, in your kitchen, even inside a prison. Consider the experience of one Florida corrections facility, which housed teenagers adjudicated as adults for various felonies, when they decided to introduce a writing program. The presence of so many violent young inmates—convicted of crimes ranging from armed robbery to rape to murder—caused prison officials to establish rules severely restricting writing and research implements. As a result, participants in the seminar were limited to only pencils and pads of paper.

Despite these restrictions, at the end of the seminar one of the instructors expressed amazement at the level of creativity the inmates had been able to express: They produced heart-wrenching autobiographical essays; poignant poems; and rather profound analyses of why they had committed their offenses and how other young people might avoid their mistakes. Some even contributed sketches to communicate their feelings and longings.

One seventeen-year-old named Eduardo drew an eye with a giant teardrop, which expressed not only his deep sorrow at being incarcerated, but also a sense of his own redemption: Reflected in the teardrop was a portrait of Jesus, dying on the cross. With nothing more than a Number 2 pencil and a piece of paper, Eduardo had exposed the depths of his heart.

Of course, I certainly never restrict myself to simple art instruments. I continue to explore more complex tools that are appearing on our most creative artistic frontiers, such as the emerging use of technology in film work. Some of the truly groundbreaking work is now being done with animated movies like *Shrek*—which has visuals and backgrounds that I drool over.

The old Disney movies, which required artists to paint each panel with painstaking effort, were beautiful works of art, which, as a onetime background painter on animated films, I can really appreciate. But advanced technology used with movies like *Shrek* can now create the same effects almost in the blink of an eye, apparently without interfering with or supplanting genuine creativity. Also, more often than not, technology has ushered in new possibilities for imagining and accomplishing objectives that might have been regarded as unattainable in the past, such as the way synthesizers revolutionized the musical arts years ago.

But despite all this progress in the development of time-saving tools, I know I'll continue to cling to the most powerful and simplest instruments of all—pencil and paper. Serious painters, writers, entrepreneurs, and other creative types always need to be prepared for serendipity—for the aesthetic muse or the divine surprise that may appear unannounced at any time or place. Ironically, though, these flashes of insight often seem to pop into mind when high-tech tools aren't readily at hand—when the personal digital assistant is in another office or the laptop device is back in the hotel room.

So even though I acknowledge that the most advanced technology can often position artists to work with greater efficiency and creative flow, I also know that we each must always expect the unexpected. For the inevitable creative surprise, I have yet to find more powerful instruments than my old-fashioned pencil and pad.

Simpler Times

VILLAGE INN

Working for Your First Love

I t's easy to get caught up in work for the sake of some final reward: a raise or promotion, the glory of raising more money for the museum than any chairperson before you, a needed paycheck, or the pride and relief of meeting a deadline.

There's nothing inherently wrong with seeking such rewards. At one time or another, each of us needs personal affirmation or money in the bank. But if the only reason you are working is for the money or accolades, you will find yourself ultimately unfulfilled. That's because a much greater reward awaits you when you are working for your "first love"— your great creative passion or calling.

A clothing designer I know in the Midwest has spent a lifetime trying to make a go of other careers. At various times, he's been a carpenter, a bank vice president, and a middle manager of a corporation. Early on in his life, he took a shot at designing clothes, but because the obstacles seemed overwhelming, he gave up his first love in order to make a living. Now, twenty years later, he's back on track, with a bold new collection of men's clothing and a gutsy determination to go forward—no matter what. I have a feeling this time he'll make it.

"Now I know what I've been missing," he says. "I used to wake up every day with a cloud over my head. Now I can't wait to start work."

My friend had a grand vision that he had tucked away someplace, a first love that he had allowed to grow cold. But as he discovered, the minute he revived the vision and began to work toward its fulfillment, something happened inside him. Working for his first love unleashed his creativity and brought him joy beyond measure—a joy that has outstripped the financial hardship and occasional rejection he endures daily in this start-up venture. As his clothing designs spring to life at his sewing machine, he can feel the pleasure—God's pleasure—in the work of his hands.

In the book of Ecclesiastes the Preacher tells us that what is good and fitting is to "find enjoyment in all the toil with which one toils under the sun the few days of his life which God has given him" (5:18 RSV). In other words, we are made to derive pleasure and fulfillment from our work, not just one or two days a year, or when a job is finished, but every day of our lives. In a way, we are meant to "live for work," especially if that work is the first love that God has implanted in our hearts.

Take Norman Rockwell, for example. He didn't just paint to live; he lived to paint, even when a particular project came hard. Consider the convoluted steps he took to achieve one of his most famous Thanksgiving covers for the *Saturday Evening Post*. In his book *My Adventures as an Illustrator*, Rockwell explained how he created drawing after drawing until he found the right configuration for the homecoming veteran and his mother seated beside the dinner table. Once he had the drawing, he sketched it out fully, and then he did an underpainting—a fully blocked-out execution of the piece. Only then did he set to work on the final version.

When the painting for the Thanksgiving cover was nearly completed, Rockwell decided that it didn't conform to the inner vision in his head. And so, with the clock ticking away on his deadline, he threw the painting away and started over, without giving it a second thought.

Rockwell was willing to sacrifice time and effort for the sake of his creative vision because the process itself was his first love. He loved the act of painting—and so do I. But even more than the act of painting, he cared about the message he was imparting through his art. If the message wasn't clear, he didn't want to let go of it until he got it right.

For me each painting is a message—a message of love from the Creator himself, funneled through my hand and shared with others. And so I continue to strive for fresh ways to satisfy the cravings for home and warmth and light that I know lie deep within the hearts of those who embrace my work. That's why I throw myself with passion into many of the marketing details involved in reproducing my paintings through my company. I see my creativity as an entrepreneur integrally linked to my creativity as an artist: Both are expressions of my first love.

From the time I asked those "What ifs?" as a young artist and discovered a way to reproduce my paintings as prints that look like oils, I've been on a twenty-plus-year quest to find definitive techniques and tools to replicate an original. Today, several innovations set my company's work apart. For one thing, we replicate the canvas on which original oil paintings are painted. In other words, our prints don't require glass covers or mats. Also, the prints often contain texture, just like an original, and are actually retouched by hand. We employ about fifty artists to do brushwork on many of our prints. In doing the highlights and other features, they use real oil paints.

In part, these transformations in the print-producing process have been driven by my belief that a painting is as close to forever as we can get on this earth, intended to be appreciated in a home by anyone who passes near it. Books stay on bookshelves. Music inspires for a few moments, but then drifts back to the CD case. As for movies, you may see a good one once; or if you buy a DVD or video, you may look at it more often. But a painting is always there—with the potential to affect sensibilities and lives for years. That's why I've paid so much attention to taking my works beyond the creation of a single original work and made it possible for millions to interact with them.

But there's more. With my paintings, I create a world that many want to enjoy in other ways, such as through home accessories, gift items, and even three-dimensional replicas made from the landscapes in my paintings. Also, there are cards, calendars, and other products that my many friends can share with others.

But underneath this "Thomas Kinkade brand," if you will, lies the basic set of questions I asked long ago, when I was just an inexperienced kid in my twenties: "How can I ensure that my paintings won't be hidden away forever in the private room of a collector who owns the actual oil? How can I replicate an original painting—and share my light-giving message with the world?"

I believe I'm beginning to answer such fundamental questions in ways that meet my original need to bring light and hope to others—and to fulfill my first vision and my first creative love.

THE SIXTH DAY
OF CREATIVE LIVING

The Cauldron of Conflict

The harder the conflict, the more glorious the triumph.

— THOMAS PAINE

COURAGE

Walking Through the Fire

or most of us, *conflict* is a dirty word, and the presence of serious conflict can be so distracting that creativity becomes impossible.

The very thought of an unexpected dispute at work, a confrontation with an obnoxious coworker on a volunteer project, or a clash with a family member makes us grow tense and anxious. Sometimes, it seems all we can think of at such times is the many ways our plans—or worse, our lives—will be ruined by these unforeseen obstacles.

Typically, we want to avoid conflict at all costs—ignore it, deny it, or run from it, rather than confront it face-to-face. Our goal is peace at any price, with the vain hope of complete harmony, gentle words, and sweet violins playing softly in the background of our lives.

But the real world isn't like that, is it? No matter how much we try to orchestrate our lives, outside pressures inevitably impinge on the perfect world we have created to jar our tranquillity and rob us of our joy. Consider some of the scenarios you, friends, or loved ones may face:

- Your fifteen-year-old son gets an F on a world history test, and your stomach balls up in a knot. *His academic life is over,* you think to yourself.
- You've organized a science workshop for one hundred kids at an environmental center, but just as the program is about to start, you discover that the bathrooms are out of order.

"You'll have to drive them a mile down the road to the public restrooms," the center's director tells you. Visions of unhappy kids, car wrecks on the way to the facilities, and lawsuits start to magnify in your brain, and you're sure disaster is imminent.

— You are about to start a new job when your father ends up in the emergency room with a stroke.

"He'll never be the man he was," the doctor says, directing you to the social worker who handles nursing homes.

Where will I get the money? you wonder. *Why is this happening to me now?*

Such difficulties may actually seem tame compared to obstacles you are facing, but they illustrate an important lesson: It's not the conflict itself that is the problem. After all, conflicts are an inevitable part of life. Rather, it's your *response* to outside challenges that can either hold you back, paralyzing you with fear and doubt, or move you forward, galvanizing you for victory.

Stop and think for a moment about the last time you faced a crisis calmly and positively. By that, I obviously don't mean that you jumped up and down for joy when the hurricane tore the roof off your house, or slapped a big grin on your face when your best friend was diagnosed with cancer. What I'm talking about is grabbing the crisis with both hands, digging in your heels, and finding a way to grow spiritually or mentally as you undergo the challenge. I'm referring to *using* the conflict to deepen your inner resources, to strengthen your will, and to push the creative envelope to expand your personal possibilities.

When I confront serious conflict in my own life, I sometimes find it reassuring to recall difficult circumstances that others have faced and surmounted. One example is the lifetime of hardships that produced the World War I American "Ace of Aces," Eddie Rickenbacker.

In 1902, he quit school at age thirteen to go to work. Because he was uneducated and unusually young, he was initially relegated to dead-end jobs and disagreeable living conditions. But rather than give up, he always saw opportunity in deprivation. While still in his mid-teens, he became the top mechanic for the Firestone car and tire company—and that was just the beginning. Every conflict, every difficult environment he faced after that became a place to grow—creatively, spiritually, and personally.

I'm always amazed, for instance, when I reflect on how well he could think and perform behind the wheel of highly dangerous and unstable racing cars. These vehicles, which rocketed along at 70 mph, were barely beyond the "horseless carriage" stage of engineering, but that didn't deter Rickenbacker. By the time he reached his twenties, he had become a national champion auto racer.

Then he switched to the machines that became his true love—the first generation of fighter planes. In the tightest and coldest cockpits of Spad and Nieuport aircraft, soaring high over France and Germany, he became the greatest American fighter ace of World War I—and a Congressional Medal of Honor winner.

But perhaps the most difficult crisis in Rickenbacker's life came aboard a life raft on the stormy Pacific during World War II. Despite the fact that he was on the outs with President Franklin D. Roosevelt when World War II broke out, Rickenbacker—then the head of Eastern Airlines—was assigned by Secretary of War Henry L. Stimson to perform secret missions abroad. While he was carrying a confidential message to General Douglas MacArthur, his aircraft went down in the Pacific. As a result, he and six companions had to fend for themselves on rafts in the open seas for twenty-four days.

For most of the ordeal, Rickenbacker, who was suffering from stiff muscles and other injuries from a previous air crash, had to remain almost immobile on a crowded life raft. Too much movement might upset the raft or cause pain to the sunburned skin of other stranded airmen.

By any measure, this crisis introduced a personal conflict of monumental proportions, a life-and-death struggle that was thrust upon him, challenging his will and ability to survive. Yet the most moving and transforming spiritual experiences of his life—indeed, perhaps the most creative expressions of his eventful life—occurred during those difficult days, when many back in the States had given him up for lost.

He delivered pep talks to his starving, water-deprived companions, led them in prayers, insisted on regular Bible readings, and encouraged the others to devise plans for signaling possible rescuers or finding food in the sea. His creative goal: to find ways to raise everyone's spirits and help all find the will to live.

Finally, an army plane picked up the survivors, and they returned home to a hero's welcome. But Rickenbacker never forgot the opportunity for personal growth he had discovered in that uncomfortable, rolling life raft. In later writings, he made it clear that being confined in that space—often on the verge of death, with thirty-foot waves, sharks, thirst, and starvation threatening from every side—produced a spiritual revolution in his life.

As Rickenbacker's experience illustrates, conflicts resulting from outside pressures are an inevitable part of every great venture, including every supremely creative effort. In fact, a life without conflict is a life divorced from reality, an existence sheltered physically, emotionally, and spiritually from the world. If we are to live fully, we must learn to expect—and even welcome—the times of crisis, believing all the while that every trial harbors the potential to realize some great creative purpose.

"When you walk through fire you shall not be burned," the book of Isaiah promises. That's the kind of hope and assurance that sustained Eddie Rickenbacker and can also enable us to rise above hard times and achieve our ultimate creative goals.

Courage

BEACON OF HOPE

The Power of Brokenness

The conflicts we are often least ready to deal with are those that involve our closest relationships. An argument with an unforgiving spouse, a rebellious child, a recalcitrant parent, or an unfaithful friend can throw us into a tailspin, leaving us shattered, hurt, and confused.

Remember the time your best friend severed your relationship over a seemingly innocuous remark you made at a dinner party?

Or what about the moment you discovered that your teenage daughter was sneaking out of the house every night and not coming back until morning?

Then there was the time your elderly father totaled his car and ended up in jail with a DUI, or the night you slipped your hand into your husband's coat pocket and unearthed a card with a handwritten phone number you didn't recognize, or . . . You can fill in the blanks as well as I.

Each of us has confronted those seemingly hopeless situations when others have let us down and we simply don't know where to turn, or whom to trust. At those moments, we may ask, "So, where's the creativity in this kind of conflict?"

I may not be able to identify one-for-one with every such problem relationship, but as the child of a broken marriage, I do know this: The fallout from a shattered personal tie can affect us for months, years, or the rest of our lives. Even so, at every step of the way, we have a choice. We can wallow in our misfortune, pining for a missing parent, an unfaithful spouse, or a wayward child. Or we can find in our brokenness a new vision for ourselves that will empower us with hope and a sense of our divine potential.

In my own case, it was my parents' divorce that triggered my creative awakening—not so much as an artist, but as a man. I can still hear the quiet but wrenching command.

"Wake up, Tommy, we're leaving."

It was three o'clock in the morning when I heard my mother's whispered order in my ear. "Let's go!" she said emphatically.

I opened my eyes in the darkness, barely able to make out her thin form leaning over me.

"Where are we going?" I asked groggily.

"To our new house," she said.

Without another word, I slipped out of bed, pulled on my clothes, tiptoed down the stairs, and followed her out the door to the car. In the backseat, still half asleep, my sister, Katey, and brother, Patrick, were waiting.

The three of us sat silently as my mother pulled away from the house and drove down the deserted street to a new life, a life without my father. At the time, I didn't really understand why or where we were going; I just followed. We left our house and went to a trailer park outside our town of Placerville, California. Two weeks after we moved into the trailer, my mom pulled me aside.

"Tommy, you're the man of the house now. Your dad's not here anymore. We've left your dad." I was six years old; my brother, Pat, was four; and my sister, Katey, thirteen.

Although I didn't know the details, I had sensed for some time that my parents' marriage was in trouble. They had been fighting a lot, and in the weeks leading up to our nighttime escape, my dad had started to get violent. Out of pure fear—for herself and for us—my mother had done the only thing she could: She picked up and left.

But first, she had turned to the Bible. As a woman of faith, she believed divorce was wrong. And yet, she was stuck in an impossible relationship with a man who was unfaithful and emotionally unstable. For guidance, she opened the Bible to the book of Jeremiah, and out popped a verse: "Flee for safety." And flee she did.

So now, here I was, a slightly pudgy, shaggy-haired six-year-old with no front tooth and a big mop of dark tousled hair—and suddenly I was expected to be a "man." It took me a while to digest what Mom had said, but it wasn't long before I grew into the job. Anytime something needed fixing around the house, I was the one to do it.

"Thom, the shingle fell off," my mom would say, and up to the roof I'd go, hammer in hand, to replace shingles.

Beyond such physical responsibilities, my new leadership role around the house had an even more profound effect on my self-image. Once I began to sense what it meant to be the man of the family, I knew that my life mattered. There was a deeper purpose to my life, a reason for my existence.

Being my mom's mainstay, I understood clearly that I wasn't here on earth just to pursue my own pleasure or to drift through life the best I could. Rather, I was here to serve others—in particular my family who, through hardship, had begun to be exceptionally bound together. I was here to be a servant, to be the bearer of God's light to the world around me, as my Sunday school teachers frequently said.

As my childhood unfolded, I had a growing sense of my own destiny as a "light-bearer." That calling on my life was so clear that by the time I was eleven, I was keeping tape-recorded journals, pronouncing solemnly into the microphone: "I know now that God has a special plan for my life."

People often ask me, "Were you prepared for success?" I believe that one of the reasons my life hasn't melted down like the lives of so many people who achieve success and renown in a certain field is that I've had some degree of preparation from day one. Ironically, the difficulties in my life provided a fundamental step toward maturity that prevented me from being too bigheaded or self-absorbed when I began entering the limelight.

As an adult, when I found myself in a position of leadership artistically, I was ready for it because of that sense of destiny that emerged in childhood. This self-awareness has nothing to do with ego or pride. In fact, it's the opposite. It's almost an extension of the phrase my mother gave me: "You're the man of the house now." The realization that my life counted was a humbling revelation, one that bore incredible responsibilities and a sense that to fulfill them, I needed only to rely on the all-powerful creativity of God.

I learned about God's creativity early on from my mother. We had moved into the little trailer with just enough money for one month's rent, but that didn't stop my mom. She believed God would provide. She lived in the realm of the miraculous and taught us to expect miracles in our own lives.

The miracles began to unfold immediately. My mom quickly landed a job as a legal secretary, and after two years in the mobile home, she bought a house with no money down, zero credit-rating, and only a brief track record at her job. She had found this little old house in the country that was up for sale for $12,000, and with the chutzpah that only a desperate single mom can muster, she went to the owner and asked, "Could you sell me the house with nothing down?"

"Do you have any collateral?" the owner asked.

"No," my mom replied. "I have my kids, and we need a place to live. But I promise I'll pay you every month."

The home owner took a chance on her, and my mom was as good as her word. It took her sixteen years, but she paid off the house—at $50 a month, plus a little more whenever she earned extra income as a notary public.

As it turned out, the house was in the best possible location for us kids growing up. It was next to the high school and right across the street from the grade school. My mom was so busy working that she could never have driven us to dances or football games. But God had provided for us, just as she had said he would, by giving us a house in the country that was not only near the schools, but also within reach of a big mountain and a forest full of oak trees, where my brother and I could let our imaginations run wild.

Even more important for me, the house was right next door to a field with an old barn that stayed empty for years. When I was thirteen, construction workers started renovating the barn and I went over to see what was happening.

"Some artist is building a studio here," said one of the workers offhandedly.

That artist turned out to be someone I introduced you to earlier—Glen Wessels, the former head of the art department at the University of

California at Berkeley and a founder of the California College of Arts and Crafts.

At the time, though, all I knew about Glen was that he was an artist, and that was enough for me. A few weeks after he moved in, I knocked on his door and asked, "Do you need any help around the studio? I'm an artist."

He took one look at me—with my bushy hair uncombed as it always was—and in a gruff voice, he brushed me off.

"I don't need any help," he said bluntly. Then he closed the door.

Talk about rejection. But a year later, something possessed me to knock on his door again, and this time, he was more welcoming.

"Hey, do you remember the last time you were here, when you asked if I needed help?" he asked.

"Yes, sir!" I replied.

"Well, I've been in an accident," he explained. "I could use someone like you around the studio."

I learned later that he had broken his hip in a Jeep accident with his friend, the famed photographer Ansel Adams. The accident had left him so immobilized that even simple tasks around the studio were too strenuous for him. Stuck out in the country with few social contacts, he had no one around who could help—that is, until I came along.

From that moment on, I became his apprentice, washing brushes, stretching his canvases, organizing his paints, and cleaning up. For two glorious hours a day, from the time I was fourteen until I graduated from high school, I rubbed shoulders with a man who is considered by many to be one of the great artistic minds of the twentieth century—all because my mom, with no credit rating, was able to buy a house near a field with a vacant old barn.

⌒

Was I broken up by my parents' divorce? Certainly. Was I destroyed? Definitely not. That's because God gave me more than one way out—a purpose as "man of the family," and a calling as an artist that was reinforced at every stage of my life. The cauldron of conflict in my own home helped me set my sights on bigger things—beyond my family, and far beyond the borders of my town.

Now, when trouble comes, I count my blessings. I've known poverty. I've known heartbreak. I've known rejection. I've seen the worst—and I know that each obstacle can be a stepping-stone to growth and blessing.

Sometimes, though, our biggest conflicts aren't imposed from the outside, or thrust upon us by our closest relationships. Instead, they come from deep within, as our creative insights struggle to break free.

Beacon of Hope

CLEARING STORMS

The Rewards of Inner Struggle

Even if we could shut ourselves off entirely from other people, we still would not be able to escape conflict.

Imagine yourself in a cabin deep in the woods, where the only sounds are the wind rustling the trees, the birds chirping, or maybe some raindrops pounding on the roof. You've arranged things so that you're all alone and can work without interruption on that special sewing project or guitar piece.

But things don't go as planned. Irritation, frustration, or anxiety intervenes unexpectedly because the valance you were designing for the window no longer seems quite so perfect. Or the melody that was flowing so effortlessly from the guitar strings becomes discordant, and no matter how hard you try, you can't quite get it right.

In such situations, the struggle doesn't come from outside pressures or personal relationships as much as from inner turmoil spawned within the creative process itself. There's no other person contributing to your discomfort, but somehow, your creative vision and rhythm are out of kilter, and you simply can't find the way to resolve the conflict.

When such inner challenges arise, how do you react? Do you fight them by throwing down your guitar in a fit of frustration, or ripping up the fabric you've been working on? Or perhaps you just dissolve in tears or go shopping.

Even the reclusive Emily Dickinson couldn't block out inner struggle. In the quietness of her garden or in her ocher brick house tucked away in Amherst, Massachusetts, her mind wrestled daily with deep spiritual issues that found their way into her poetry. Death, life, heaven, hell—the most profound conflicts of all were challenges she willingly accepted as part of her creative calling.

Taking a cue from the Belle of Amherst, I've found that the most productive first step in dealing with inner conflict is to just *accept it as a fact of the creative life*. Instead of fighting against those inevitable disruptive feelings, I try to embrace them.

I may try to objectify the threatening worry or distraction by treating it as though it were some irritating human visitor knocking on my door.

"Oh, so here you are again," I may say to the mental intruder.

Then, I'll sit quietly for a time and bide my time until the uninvited guest decides to leave. More often than not, just waiting quietly for a few minutes is all that's necessary to cause the unwelcome emotion or sense of conflict to fade away—and allow my mind to settle down so that creative ideas can begin to percolate once again.

By now, I've grown so accustomed to creative conflict when I'm all alone that I'm ready for it. I know that when I hit a snag in a painting, if I exercise some patience, the solution will usually come. Sometimes it takes minutes, sometimes weeks, and on rare occasions, the waiting period may be months. But I know that eventually the right idea will bubble up from the cauldron of creative conflict inside me.

Typical of how this works for me was a challenge I faced when I was working on a particular painting of a garden scene several years ago. I was barely twenty minutes into the painting when the crisis hit. Earlier that morning, I came up with what I thought would be the perfect balance for the composition: The vanishing point—or central focus that draws the viewer's eye into the distance—would lie just off to the left, beyond a cluster of overgrown trees.

With this organizing principle in mind, I used hues of blue to draw my first lay-in, or sketch, for the landscape. But just as I was ready to start adding the layers of color that would bring the painting to life, I realized something was terribly wrong. Despite my vision of what the scene *should* have looked like—despite the game plan I had carefully laid out in my mind—I saw as I worked that my approach to the composition wasn't in balance at all.

There was no point in moving ahead on this track, and so I put down my brush and stewed for a few minutes. It didn't help my mood that the scene looked unorganized and messy, and that I knew my creative moment was facing a challenge. Then, I took a deep breath, said a silent prayer, and sat quietly and serenely, with less regard to the time pressures.

If this doesn't work out today, there's always tomorrow, I thought.

Then, without warning, everything came together. I introduced the compositional device of a weathered stone bridge, and suddenly a new emotional depth entered the scene. That small but profound detail was all I needed to get back on my creative track. Soon the simple garden image was transformed by an act of intuitive faith and a landmark new work, *The Bridge of Faith* (an apt enough title, considering the circumstances of its creation), was born.

A painting—like any other creative challenge—can be a wily opponent. Like a tough competitor in a championship chess match, it can create unforeseen obstacles that can stop the flow of the game—unless the artist learns to bend and adjust when conflict strikes.

The great American painter Andrew Wyeth encountered such an opponent in *Christina's World,* his almost photographic tempera painting of a young woman sitting in a bleak field looking toward a small house on a hill. The painting was nearly finished when Wyeth realized it wasn't working. The scene was dead . . . lifeless . . . devoid of any sense of humanity.

After delaying for days, he finally found the creative solution: He would paint Christina's dress pink. With just a few brushstrokes, including the merest blush of color on her dress, he transformed the painting into a masterpiece, a classic of American art. Seeing how his once lifeless scene now leaped and vibrated with vitality, Wyeth knew instantly what a great artistic feat he had accomplished.

The lesson for you? If you feel things are not going right creatively in a particular project, it's often better just to stop and wait for a while instead of proceeding on the wrong track.

Also, this wait-and-see approach to inner conflict applies to most other fields of activity and work. I'm reminded of Will, an entrepreneur specializing in health and fitness products, who underwent tremendous turmoil after he had made a dramatic decision to pour an unusual amount of cash from his savings accounts and credit lines into a new venture—a unique and untried form of Internet marketing.

The idea for the new concept had popped into Will's head during one of his daily workouts on a stationary bike in a local gym. But before leaping into action, he spent considerable time over a period of several weeks analyzing the pros and cons of the move. Finally, he concluded that despite the need to commit so much money to the new concept, the risks were worth the potential reward.

But after he spent the funds, the approaching deadlines for paying his employees and meeting other financial obligations confronted him in fresh, nerve-racking clarity. He worried that if the cash from the new venture didn't come in as expected, he might find himself in serious financial trouble: the very existence of his business might be in jeopardy.

"I found myself waking up in the middle of the night shaking, in a cold sweat," he recalled. "Then I couldn't get back to sleep. Possible disaster scenarios kept running through my mind, and I simply couldn't shut them off."

As a result of the high anxiety and the chronic fatigue Will experienced from a lack of rest, he was unable to think creatively about his pending Internet concept. Even though he knew the venture required further adjustments and revisions, he simply couldn't focus his mind on the issue. As a result, he became more and more anxious and conflicted.

As his panic mounted, Will tried to bring God into the picture by setting aside some time each day to ask for divine guidance and help. But ironically, the more he pressured himself in prayer to "quit obsessing over financial deadlines and finish up your work!" the more anxious, preoccupied, and uncreative he felt.

Finally, he *gave up*—literally threw up his hands and told himself, "Okay, if you're going to fall flat on your face and go out of business, so be it!"

Then, as a kind of afterthought, he looked up and prayed, "Lord, is this really what you want? Do you want me to fail? Well, it's up to you now, because I'm at the end of my rope. It's not my will but yours."

That was exactly the mind-set Will needed to begin to resolve his inner conflict and turmoil. After he acknowledged to God and to himself that, if necessary, he could accept the absolute worst-case scenario, a new perspective emerged. He realized that even though it wasn't his first choice, he could withstand the blow to his pride and pocketbook if he had to lay off most or all of his employees. And if he had to go into another line of work to support his family, that was possible, too. He still had his natural creativity and finely honed advertising skills, and one way or another, he would survive—and maybe even thrive.

As Will's mind and spirit finally broke free, he began to feel a deep sense of peace and equilibrium. The agonizing inner conflict that had raised the prospect of utter failure and rejection no longer had any power over him. Just as important, the internal battles he had been forced to fight actually transformed him into a stronger person.

Although Will might have felt at first that he was wrestling with an all-powerful angel of anxiety and fear, in the end, he prevailed. Not only did he triumph over his inner problem, but he also saw his business gradually move to a firmer financial footing. And in the wake of this victory, he learned that even the most difficult and excruciating inner struggle can indeed produce a great reward.

VICTORIAN LIGHT

Besieged

Sometimes, our creativity is blocked because we feel besieged on all sides, not only from within, but also from without. Deadline pressures, financial difficulties, or demanding employees or coworkers may be squeezing your mind like a vise.

You've been there, haven't you? I know I have, and so has a woman whom I'll call Marsha. One time, she spent most of a year organizing a trunk show as a fund-raiser for her daughter's school, but then disaster struck a week before the event. Her daughter came down with the flu, her consultant husband lost a big contract, and her most popular trunk-show vendor bowed out, leaving her desperate for a replacement.

In the throes of these conflicts, Marsha felt as though she had joined Han Solo, Luke Skywalker, and Princess Leia in *Star Wars* when they were trapped inside a giant garbage compactor on the evil Death Star. Every morning when she awoke, she sensed she was drowning in some sort of mental or emotional muck. Inner walls were closing in minute by minute, and there appeared to be no way out.

Seemingly blocked on all sides, panic-stricken, and nearly crushed emotionally from fatigue, she finally asked no one in particular, "What do I do now?"

That one question was all she needed to penetrate the inner barrier. Now, Marsha found that she was free to start confronting the core issues.

"Stop for a minute and think," she said to herself. "This isn't the biggest crisis you've ever faced in your life, is it? You've dealt with other problems, and you can deal with this one."

But Marsha didn't just sit there and wait for creative lightning to strike. She knew that for her, when a block appears, that's a good time to forge ahead and keep working.

Like Marsha, I know that even when I'm besieged by multiple challenges professionally and personally, with enough time and effort I can work through them. In fact, I now can say with some confidence that I really don't have artist's block anymore because for me, a "block" is not really a block at all. Rather, it's an opportunity to apply renewed effort and more imagination to a problem, such as the one I faced not long ago when I was working on my painting *City by the Bay, Sunset on Fisherman's Wharf, San Francisco.*

At the time, I was under tremendous pressure from my business associates to get this painting done—not merely to finish it, but to make it a blockbuster. In effect, as so often happens, I had to produce a blockbuster "on demand." Day after day, I would walk into my studio feeling like Barry Bonds stepping up to the plate. I knew I had to hit a home run. I couldn't settle for a bunt or a line drive or a sacrifice fly. I needed an out-and-out homer. That's the kind of pressure I felt for six long weeks, and at times, the weight of responsibility was unbearable.

"You can't get it done," I'd hear a little voice whisper in my ear, and I'd find myself getting anxious, worrying, dreaming about the painting day and night. I never doubted that I would get it finished, but the question was *When?*

I had faced this kind of problem before. When a painting is in its "ugly" phase, it's like life in its ugly phase. All you can do is stand up to it and fight. And so, I kept plugging away.

Some days I'd go to the studio and try to force it. When nothing worked, I found myself looking at the floor blankly, thinking, *This thing looks so bad. Help me, Lord.*

Little by little, the help came. The painting moved forward—inch by inch at times—but forward, nonetheless. Finally, it was finished. I turned it over to my assistant, who whisked it out of the studio and sent it over to our publishing facilities.

The minute the painting was out of my hands, I felt a tremendous weight lift from my shoulders, and I erupted with creative syncretism. As

I walked through my studio, every book I touched, every piece of music I heard, triggered a new idea for a painting or a business concept. Over the next three days, I organized the marketing rollout for my next six print releases. I took a painting that was going nowhere and whipped it into shape. I conceptualized an entirely new series of paintings.

It was a strange, giddy time of explosive creativity, a nonstop flow of free association, punctuated by one epiphany after another. That three-day power surge unleashed a creative flow that continued unabated for many weeks—all because I had stuck with it and pushed through my struggle with *Fisherman's Wharf.*

But as most hard workers know, the experience of feeling "blocked" or stymied creatively—and the inner conflict or sense of dislocation that accompanies such a block—can be a multifaceted phenomenon. Sometimes, just waiting for the block to disappear or attempting to push through it with more work doesn't do the job. In fact, such responses may make matters worse. In these situations, I'll often resort to a response that I call "thinking outside the palette."

CONQUERING THE STORMS

Thinking Outside the Palette

Perhaps the most creative strategy to escape from a creative conflict is to *leap*—mentally, emotionally, and spiritually— out of your current stale, uninspired reality into an entirely different mind-set or imaginative dimension.

So how might this work in practice? The basic idea is to take some extraordinary, even radical, step that will help break the internal shackles and help you start thinking and working "outside the box" again. Or to put the cliché in painter-ese, when I'm in a real creative bind, I look for dramatic ways to "think outside the palette."

One effective technique may be simply to leave the office or studio for a few hours, or even a day or so, and try something entirely new. Take the experience of Charlotte Terry, a successful Florida real-estate executive, who wrestles daily with the challenges of a notoriously high-stress business: She finds a creative outlet in improving the lives of others.

On any given day, Charlotte may do what absolutely must be done to keep her business going and her clients satisfied, and then execute a 180-degree about-face to focus on one of her many service projects. She might plunge into running the Girl Scout troop she organized in the local African-American community. Or she might organize a fund-raiser for her pet literary project, the Laura Riding Jackson Foundation. Or she could open her fish camp at pristine Blue Cypress Lake to a group of local artists for a day of plein air painting.

Because Charlotte refuses to allow thorny work issues to generate unnecessary tension (she approaches every obstacle as a problem to be solved, rather than as a deal-breaking crisis), her mind usually remains free to produce a constant cascade of creative ideas, for both her business and her philanthropic projects. Paradoxically, by the way, in devoting strategic chunks of her time to nonwork projects, she actually enhances her ability to do her job better. She regularly involves her clients in her service projects, so that her work and "good works" become intertwined. And more often than not, when she's working with her Girl Scouts or gazing out at a scene on the lake, a new real-estate idea will strike, or a solution to a problem faced by one of her clients will crystallize.

As for me, when I find myself stymied or stale from excessive work conflicts, I put my creativity to work in other venues. A few months ago, the out-of-the-palette response I chose was to build a chicken coop. You heard that right: I built the most upscale chicken coop you ever saw, right next to the little building that serves as my conference room and just around the corner from the studio where I paint.

Just designing and building the coop were therapeutic for me, but I've discovered some unexpected ongoing benefits. Now, whenever I need a change of pace, I head for that chicken coop to collect eggs. The minute I walk in, I'm assaulted by a chorus of clucks and the aroma of fresh hay and feathers. For five minutes or so, I move from hen to hen, deftly retrieving the newly laid eggs from under each puffy breast.

In the back of my mind, I'm dreaming of a fabulous ending for those eggs: eggs Benedict for breakfast . . . deviled eggs for lunch . . . one of Nanette's tasty cakes for dessert at dinner.

But there's more to this than simply stimulating my culinary imagination. In some way I can't quite explain, the chicken coop stimulates me to think creatively about a broad swath of issues and topics—the comforts of a traditional rural home, my connection to other living creatures, the importance of our personal links to the land.

In that coop, I feel the romance of farm life, with its bucolic rhythms of plantings and seasons. I picture cows and fields and tractors. I see the farmer pitching hay into a barn, his wife baking an apple pie, and his son raising pigs for the county fair. Most of all, I see values—solid American values of hard work, simplicity, and shared purposes.

My imagination comes to life in new, unanticipated ways in my chicken coop. In fact, the fresh creative stimulation makes me think that one of these days, those coop-inspired images might make their way into a painting or two. But for the moment, the coop just helps me get out of a rut; it revives my creative juices and enables me to "think outside the palette" once again.

THE SEVENTH DAY OF CREATIVE LIVING

The Spirit of Worship

Let us offer to God acceptable worship, with reverence and awe; for our God is a consuming fire.

— HEBREWS 12:28–29 RSV

Yosemite Valley

Magic Mountains

Finally, we have reached the last day in our exploration of creativity—the Seventh Day, which is the ancient day of rest. The creative impulse continues to throb, but under the surface and subconsciously.

To achieve the highest possible level of creativity on the other six days, we must turn our attention elsewhere on this Seventh Day of Creative Living. Our eyes focus on broader concerns, on higher matters, on God himself. For it is only by periodically diverting our eyes from our creative goals that we can hope to achieve those goals.

So what does it mean in practical terms to turn our attention away from ourselves and our cherished goals on this Seventh Day?

The first operative principle is to grasp that true worship—the worship that undergirds and inspires all creativity—is *infinitely expansive*. The very word *worship* invokes images of something great and powerful, something of surpassing worth, of those things that we esteem, revere, and honor beyond all else.

Our language is replete with references to worship. We talk about hero worship, worshiping the almighty dollar, worshiping the ground someone walks on. No less a philosopher than Thoreau used the term to inveigh against the nineteenth-century trend to worship "fashion," as he put it.

Implicit in each of these references is an understanding that the object of our worship, whatever or whoever it may be, commands our uttermost obedience and devotion. Worship isn't something we do halfheartedly. Whether we worship mammon, or beauty, or a lover, or ourselves, we give ourselves over to its all-encompassing power.

It's not so surprising, then, that the worship of God has been understood historically as an act of abject servitude. In biblical terms, the Hebrew and Greek words for *worship* refer to the work of slaves or servants. We are expected to come to God as a slave would to a master, prostrating ourselves at his feet, fully cognizant of the magnitude of his power.

But how do we get to the point where we are ready to prostrate ourselves before the Almighty, to offer "acceptable worship," as the book of Hebrews puts it? How can we separate ourselves from our own labors and egos to be as awestruck in the face of God as the shepherds were in that field in Bethlehem, or as Moses was on Mount Horeb? We have no angelic herald or burning bush to send us to our knees, shrinking in fear and wonder at the awesome power of God.

Or do we?

At our very fingertips are "magic mountains," those majestic peaks of recognition that trigger in us a sense of who God is and what he wants from us. For me, those "magic mountains" aren't far away. Rather, they are right in my own backyard in California, where, to paraphrase the psalmist, it seems the trees of the wood rejoice and the mountains skip like rams.

So when I hear the word *worship*, my mind automatically turns to the beauty of the natural world—the babbling brooks, golden fields, roaring oceans, twinkling stars, and soaring mountains. Overall, the evidence of God's creativity is almost too overwhelming for me to comprehend.

As an artist, I see in each rosebud or each speck of sand the hand of One whose palette is infinite and whose vision is beyond imagining. From the heights of the Rockies, where alpine flowers peek out from the tundra, to the depths of the Pacific, where luminescent jellyfish light up the darkness with flashes of neon, God offers us daily a glorious witness to his power and majesty.

At such wonders, all I can do is bow down in awe. In our very midst, the earth paints a portrait of the beauty and goodness God has in store for us in his everlasting kingdom. All nature is his canvas, a brilliant testament to the magnificence of our present creative potential and of the heavenly home that awaits us.

But of all nature's wonders, it is the mountains that beckon me most. In the thrusting strength of the Jungfrau, the white-capped summits of the High Sierra, or the symmetrical slopes of Fujiyama, I hear the echo of God's Spirit. For me, these earthly peaks are a foretaste of the indescribable joy and power that can be ours when we approach "Mount Zion . . . the city of the living God, the heavenly Jerusalem," as the book of Hebrews (12:22 RSV) describes the realm of the Almighty.

That power, that strength, that sense of wonder at God's holy presence is what consumed me one day nearly twenty years ago, when I first saw the mountains that changed my life. I was between classes at Berkeley searching for a touch of inspiration, when I wandered into the Oakland Museum of Art. Typically, in a free moment like this, I would have been standing in front of my easel painting furiously. But over the previous few weeks, my subjects had become stale, dry, and lifeless, and I could feel myself getting more and more edgy.

It was mid-morning and the museum was practically empty as I wandered aimlessly from gallery to gallery, without any particular purpose. Every now and then, my eye would fall on a painting and I would stop for a moment and analyze the technique. Here was an Edgar Payne, a plein air painting awash in a blizzard of small dots of vivid color that came together in an impressionistic California country scene. There was a Charles Christian Nahl, a marvel of expressive action that brought the Gold Rush days to life. Each one had something to tell me, and as politely as I could, I tried to listen.

But I couldn't focus. My mind was far away, still searching for something as yet unseen. After an hour or so, I was about to pick up and leave when I turned the corner into the main gallery of nineteenth-century landscape art.

Dominating the far wall, a monumental painting of Yosemite Valley set against a sheer mountain mise-en-scène left me speechless. I could feel the hair on my arms tingling.

How was the artist able to create this? It was the same question I had asked myself as a seven-year-old kid in the gallery on Fisherman's Wharf, only this time I actually knew something about painting.

Flush with exhilaration, I walked closer to the painting to read the inscription on a little brass plate on the frame: "*The Yosemite Valley,* Thomas Hill, 1829–1908."

Off to the right, a plaque on the wall gave further explanation: "Thomas Hill, known as the 'Artist of Yosemite,' was considered one of the most prominent American landscape painters of his time. His best-known work, *Driving the Last Spike,* celebrated the joining of the Union-Pacific Railroad. During his lifetime, he painted more than five thousand paintings of Yosemite."

I took a step back from the painting and marveled. I had never seen a more compelling illusion of the third dimension on any painted surface. What astonished me was the way Hill had created a sense of depth through a masterful manipulation of light. As his objects receded into the distance, they became grayer, merging into a primeval haze. Light became dark and dark became light, in an almost mystical communion of inter-locking color.

My eyes followed the river through the carved mountain pass far into the violet haze, and before long I was no longer in a museum looking at a mounted painting. Instead, I was physically in the painting. I could feel the early morning mist on my face and sense the awesome power of the mountains towering over me.

I wanted to stay in that place forever. It was a region redolent of pine and oaks and fresh breezes, a microcosm of the High Sierra, the mountain range that had provided the backdrop for my childhood. Growing up in Placerville, I could often glimpse the white-capped summits of the crystal range of the Sierras pointing heavenward. The image had so fired my imagination that from then on, the very sight of a mountain aroused my creative passion.

The mountains became a natural metaphor for God, a mantle covering me with total security and warmth. They were timeless, eternal, an all-enveloping Father figure that hovered protectively.

As I stood there in that museum staring at Thomas Hill's *Yosemite,* the mountains again ignited my imagination, and once more I could feel the adrenaline pumping.

Nature in its most grand—that's what I want to paint! That's it!

Like a wound-up spring, I bounded out of the Oakland Museum, fixated on my mission. From then on, Berkeley and its emphasis on modernism couldn't contain me. I switched schools and went to Pasadena, where the Art Center College of Design carried me closer to my vision of creating landscape art.

From that moment on, I pursued my art with even greater passion, painting visionary landscapes that represented my own expression of the worshipful awe I felt inside. And it all started with those mountains.

What are your magic mountains? What are the sights and sounds that bring you to your knees with hands outstretched in awesome wonder? Is it the rosy face of your three-year-old asleep in her bed? Is it the hug of a student whose life God has privileged you to touch? Is it the rhythmic pulses of a jazz piano composition? Is it the intricate hand-stitching of an early American quilt or the graceful curve of a long-stemmed rose clipped from your prize garden?

I challenge you today to open your eyes and behold your magic mountains—the interludes of divine light that lead you heavenward. Then lift up your hands and give God acceptable worship, with thanks in your heart to the One who is Lord of all. Take time regularly to wander freely in your place of inspiration and delight. Head to your mountains, for it is there that your strength is restored.

ALMOST HEAVEN

Contemplating David

The most creative worship is rooted in humility.

Our capacity to worship God sincerely begins when we empty ourselves of self-pride. We are so busy setting goals, and achieving, and filling our palm pilots with "to do" lists that we forget we are not really the ones "doing the doing."

But no matter how successful we may be as parents, businesspeople, musicians, or friends, at some point in our lives we come up against something beyond our ability to control. Perhaps it's a rebellious teenager, a serious illness, or a business deal that's going south.

Whatever the obstacle, it pits us against an unknown fate, leaving us unsure of ourselves and the capabilities we had grown to trust. It is only then, when we come face-to-face with our own weaknesses, that we can take on the giants. Our vulnerability brings us to a point where we can finally understand that we are merely vessels, instruments waiting to be filled with God's infinite, creative power.

"All things are possible with God," the Bible says (Mark 10:27 RSV). It doesn't say, "All things are possible with Thom," or "All things are possible in my own strength." As I've found again and again in my life, the source of true confidence isn't in ourselves, but in the Author of creativity himself.

David understood this even as a shepherd boy, and therein lay his strength. He wasn't merely brash and reckless, a cocky kid filled with confidence that he could make the shot with his sling and take down the evil enemy Goliath. Sure, he had chased lions and bears and caught them by their beards and killed them flat out. David was confident in what he could do; but he was even more confident in God: "The LORD will deliver you into my hand," he told Goliath (1 Sam. 17:46 RSV). And so God did, with great creativity. He put into David's head the preposterous idea that with one smooth stone he could slay a giant.

David's true heroism was his humility. He knew he was merely an instrument in the divine scheme of things, and he was bold enough to risk his life to let God work through him. His humility was an act of worship.

Michelangelo understood this when he carved the monumental statue of David that stands in the Gallery of the Academy in Florence. I saw Michelangelo's *David* for the first time a few years ago, and it was an earth-shaking experience. As I stood before the towering, muscular figure, which was completed when Michelangelo was only twenty-nine years old, I was awestruck by the artist's passion—not only for his art, but also for his faith.

Michelangelo doesn't portray David as a conquering hero, with his arm back, ready to throw the stone. Instead, his *David* stands in a moment of reflection. His eyes are resolute, but the sling sits softly in hand, resting momentarily on his shoulder.

This *David* is like the pitcher on the mound, caught in a moment of classic doubt. It's the last inning of the World Series, and you're up one run with the bases loaded.

"Can I pull this off?" he seems to be saying. "Can I make the pitch?" Without God's help, he might not be able to come through.

We know what happens next, and yet what makes this *David* so inspiring is that he's so like us. He's not yet the conqueror who later cuts off the Philistine's head in triumph. Although he's physically commanding, in his hesitation he's merely a man, an authentic human being touched by a twinge of doubt.

"David with the sling, I with the bow, Michelangelo," the sculptor once said, comparing himself and his sculpting tool to the biblical hero (see "Selected References," Elsen, 1967, 148). But as Michelangelo communicates so subtly through the statue of David, the work of his hands isn't just his work—it is God's artistry through him. The statue is the artist's humble offering—an ultimate act of worship that stands as a testament to the creative power of God.

You may not have a sculptor's talent to transform a block of marble into a masterpiece, or an entrepreneur's knack at building a business, or a coach's ability to motivate a team of twelve-year-old soccer players. But you do have something to offer: yourself. Wherever you are in your life right now, whatever challenges you may be facing, you can adopt an attitude of expectant humility.

It's an approach I take every day of my life. From the moment I wake up, I turn to God in prayerful anticipation, knowing that each new day and each new crisis brings the potential for divinely inspired creativity. Down deep I know that I'm not the one who creates my paintings, just as David wasn't the one who killed Goliath. I am merely a man with limited human skills who is waiting to be empowered.

Will you let God empower you—today? Humble yourself before him, and expect the giants to fall.

THE GARDEN OF PRAYER

The Garden of Prayer

reative worship arises from a state of profound balance—a communion with God so intense that we find ourselves in complete harmony with the elemental forces of the universe. In that place of supreme equipoise, we find tranquillity and an ineffable peace. "The LORD of hosts is with us; the God of Jacob is our refuge," the psalmist wrote (46:7 NKJV).

There are times in life when we understand this truth without a shadow of doubt. This happened to my friend Marie when she was sitting in a hospital room next to the bed of her brother, Robert, who was dying of a brain tumor. They had been chatting quietly, when she noticed his face starting to contort in a seizure. Her first instinct was fear, and so she shouted for a doctor. But while she was waiting for the physician to arrive, panic gave way to prayer, and soon Marie sensed a presence in the room so powerful that she actually began to feel an abiding sense of peace.

Her brother felt it, too. Moments later his seizure stopped, and, looking at her with a smile, he said, "Thank you for being here."

Marie smiled back, knowing with assurance that in some way she might never understand, her life and her brother's were in perfect balance through God's love. In some mysterious, even mystical way, they were part of his grand design.

The sense of divine order Marie connected to through prayer that day isn't merely an abstract concept, nor is it limited to the nonrational, spiritual realm. Rather, the balance she felt also underlies the physical creation and may actually be reflected in mathematical principles of perfect or near-perfect balance known variously as the Golden Section, the Golden Mean, or Divine Proportion. The Golden Mean is actually a specific ratio that expresses the relationship of one part to the other.

The medieval Italian mathematician Leonardo of Pisa, also known as "Fibonacci," and the Renaissance scholar Luca Pacioli both added to our understanding of this fundamental concept. Although the math gets rather complex, you can think of the Golden Section in terms of a simple ratio. For ideal balance and aesthetic pleasure, when a structure is divided into two parts, the short part should have the same ratio to the longer as the longer has to the whole. That "Golden Number," or ratio of the smaller to the larger part, is approximately 1.6180 expressed as a quotient.

Why is this concept of the Golden Section or Golden Number so important?

In the creation of art, a major reason to design according to the Golden Section is that for many and perhaps most of us, the resulting balance produces maximum aesthetic pleasure. It's easier to look at the painting or architectural structure, to enjoy it, and ultimately to enter and explore it. The structure of the Greek Parthenon, as well as many of the paintings of Masters like Leonardo da Vinci and the impressionist Georges Seurat, was designed to conform to the Golden Section. And underlying structure is a major factor in our looking upon these works as great art.

But perhaps there is more to all this than just mathematical formulas, geometric balance, and a pleasant emotional response to artwork. In fact, mathematicians and other scientists after Fibonacci and Pacioli found that the Golden Section, Golden Mean, and Golden Number—and the math that undergirds these concepts—can be found throughout nature. A number of journal articles and treatises have been written showing that many flower petals, animal reproductive cycles, leaf buds, and even vast cosmic nebulae are organized around the principle of the Golden Section and Number.

It has become increasingly clear, then, that the Golden Section and the math associated with it aren't just some human concoction. Rather, there seem to be universal mathematical proportions that underlie the very fabric of creation. Again, we have more than a hint of the masterful work of God the Creator and Artist—who is also the Master Mathematician.

Finally, what does all this mean for me, an artist who strives above all to capture something of God's creative method and vision in his work? The simple meaning is this: I know that to draw viewers into my paintings in an attitude of worship—to touch a deep chord in them and perhaps change their lives—I must, whenever possible, rely on universal, divine principles such as the Golden Mean. And that brings me to my 1997 painting *The Garden of Prayer,* which depicts a neoclassical gazebo situated between a peacefully flowing stream and a lazily winding country path.

I believe one of the major reasons this has become one of my most popular paintings, with numbers of people finding it eminently comforting to them, is that the structure of the painting conforms to the Golden Section. In *The Garden of Prayer,* mathematical and spiritual principles are inextricably intertwined.

As I began to work on this project, I went through my usual underdrawing and massing—all the while imagining and experimenting with different shapes and organizational concepts that I thought might become the focus of the final painting. Finally, slightly to the right of the canvas center, I sketched in the gazebo. A rather large structure, it eventually became the central focus of the scene. Here, individual imagination could find a quiet, serene place to commune with Something beyond itself.

But I knew that prayer isn't a static activity. Although we may sit, kneel, stand, or prostrate ourselves in one place before the Almighty, the extra-dimensional probes that emanate from the mind and spirit finally enter distant realms that we can never completely understand. So prayer might begin in the gazebo and its serene garden, but it certainly couldn't end there.

To suggest the mysterious movement and power of spiritual communication—and at the same time draw the viewer into the depths of the painting—I created two strong, vertical paths of light. The one on the left began in a bright haze in the sky and descended to follow the path of a bright but quiet, downward-flowing stream. The vertical shaft on the right followed a winding path that began at the base of the canvas, meandered through shimmering grass and soft shadows, and finally ended in a subtle, twinkling column that thrust the eye toward the upper part of the canvas.

But even though I had designed the painting to suggest up-and-down movement, with a hint of the hazy, bright spiritual unknown on each side, the dominant path that you'll most likely take when you enter this painting is more elliptical. You'll enter the path at a point outside the painting—along the unseen line of an ellipse that enters the canvas at the bottom to join with the winding path on the right. But before you exit at the top on the right side, a strong series of curving shapes will draw your eye back across the painting toward the left side.

Those who study *The Garden of Prayer* closely will see, first of all, two strong, elliptical shapes that serve as the base for the gazebo. The curved dome of the structure echoes those shapes and also pulls the eye over from the winding path, across the bright, pink-flowering trees, and then down again into the left vertical shaft, which is marked by the quietly flowing stream.

Natural ellipses, delineated by the outward-curving stream on the left side and the path on the right, reinforce this circular eye movement. As a result, the interplay of aesthetics and mathematics enables you to take both a physical and a spiritual journey inside *The Garden of Prayer.*

A physical tour of the painting is designed to produce a quiet, restful, stress-free amble through an idealized landscape. Yet toward the end of the path on the right and in the bright haze above the stream on the left, the mystical and the unknown take over. The prayers originating in the gazebo have now moved outside the realms of time and space to someplace in the unseen distance, where faith and serendipity reign. Finally, after you've been satisfied spiritually, you'll return on the left, down the sparkling stream, until you finally flow out of the painting with the stream that spills off the canvas on the bottom left.

As you plunge into your own creative work, you may not be as focused on geometric ratios as I am. But be assured that as you sculpt or design interiors or otherwise pursue creativity in various areas of your life, principles of balance are likely to be at work. The more you study and prepare, the more adept you'll become at recognizing and using these creative mechanisms—and the more ready you'll be to leap into realms of worship that can't be fully understood.

The Garden of Prayer

SPRING GATE

Biker Faith

True worship is total abandonment.

There are lots of ways to express this abandonment in terms of postures or physical responses. You can do it on your knees in the privacy of your bedroom. You can do it standing up waving a hanky in a packed auditorium. You can do it on a five-hundred-mile pilgrimage in Spain or in Notre Dame or at the Wailing Wall. You can do it singing or laughing or weeping or dancing. You can do it reciting a liturgy or writing a poem or yes, painting a painting.

Creativity itself is an act of worship, an ultimate expression of the gifts God has bestowed on us. If we are created in his image, we are born to express ourselves with boundless imagination, especially in our style of worship.

But most of us don't bring physical and emotional creativity into our worship lives. We merely accept the way things have been done in our families and in our congregations year after year, without wondering if this is the utmost and highest God has for us. We become stale, tired, and bored, and inexorably the faith of our fathers and mothers grows weak and powerless. In an effort to bring excitement into our lives, we turn instead to other things to get charged up—to TV reality shows, the Super Bowl, the mall—anyplace where things seem to be engaged and active.

But if you dig deep within, you may find yourself yearning for a new beginning with God. You may find yourself wanting to be back in his fold, not in the old way—marching to the beat of some staid drummer—but in an electrifying new way that expresses who you truly are. You want to let go of the trappings of religion to tap into the spiritual freedom that you sense is somewhere out there waiting for you. You want to live life with no holds barred, free from anxiety over the mortgage, your father's stroke, the leaky roof, terrorist attacks, your kid's failing grades, your spouse's new business venture, or your son's rocky marriage.

In short, you want to be free to live on the cutting edge of life's adventure, feeling dynamic new power bursting forth in your life moment by moment as each new experience becomes charged with God's all-consuming passion for living.

I know how you feel, because I've been there.

Despite my responsible life as a father, husband, and good citizen, a part of me has been a biker at heart—not just any biker, but rather, a Harley-driving, hair swept back, leather-wearing kind of biker. When I'm roaring down the road, I sometimes feel like I have let go completely, releasing the creative energy that is pent up inside me waiting to explode.

Back in art school in Pasadena, I could feel the creative volcano building. I was doing what I wanted to do—studying classical art—but my heart was painfully restless. I felt like a caged lion, pacing back and forth with nowhere to run.

It never dawned on me that my perennial restlessness might have something to do with God. I had been a faithful churchgoer in high school, but all through Berkeley and art school, I had been so impassioned about painting and studying that I put my spiritual life on the back burner. From time to time I had given God a nod by dropping in at a Christian fellowship group at art school. But even that wasn't satisfying, especially when I heard my fellow Christian artists saying things such as, "My art is just a way to pay the bills. My real ministry is working with kids at the church."

Though I totally respect such selfless dedication, some part of me felt completely out of sync with such sentiments. I couldn't shake the idea that for me, art was more than a job: It was really a calling. All my life I had sensed that calling, but now I was beginning to get confused. If God had a purpose for my life, as I had always believed, then somehow my art and my purpose must be related. But if so, how?

I'm not sure what drew me to that revival meeting one spring night in Pasadena. Maybe it was an unconscious craving to answer some of these deep personal questions. Or maybe it was the comments I had heard about the fiery minister who was coming to preach. Or maybe it was the cute girl from class who had invited me there. Whatever the reason, I found myself sitting in a huge auditorium surrounded by a type of Christian I had never encountered before.

Like the rough-and-tumble bikers I occasionally encountered on my periodic road trips, these Christians weren't the least bit dignified—at least not the way churchgoers had been at the little country church where I worshiped growing up in Placerville. These people were loud. Boisterous. They raised their hands. They shouted out spontaneous praises. They tapped their toes and sang at the top of their lungs.

This was "radical faith," the real deal, practiced by down-to-earth people who were as passionate about their God as a biker is about his hog. These people loved God to such a degree that it spilled out of their mouths and came out through their arms and feet.

I wanted what they had. In that auditorium I could feel the raucous presence of God, and I had a sense that he was going to meet me there that very night. For about an hour, I sat through the service, soaking up the Spirit. I wasn't yet ready to lift my hands or shout out praises, but as I heard the old familiar songs, my heart began to stir.

"O Lord my God! When I in awesome wonder . . . Consider all the worlds Thy hands have made . . ."

My mind flooded with images—the High Sierra . . . the Pacific Coast . . . Yosemite Valley. These were God's landscapes, monuments of breathtaking beauty designed by the Creator himself to draw me deep into his canvas, into the artistry of his world.

"I see the stars, I hear the rolling thunder, Thy pow'r throughout the universe displayed . . ."

The natural world is a gift, God's incredible gift to me, I thought to myself. On this earthly canvas, God had crafted soaring mountains, bubbling brooks, and towering redwoods. He had created lightning and thunder and skies brushed with sunsets ablaze with pinks and oranges and blues.

He had created all of it for my eye to see and my soul to rejoice.

"Then sings my soul, my Savior God, to Thee, How great thou art! . . ."

I had heard these verses hundreds of times before in church or while watching Billy Graham crusades on television, but they had never penetrated my soul the way they did now.

The music swelled to a crescendo, and as I rose to my feet, I heard the sound of my own voice belting out the chorus:

"How great thou art! How great thou art!"

As the words poured out of my mouth, my entire body responded at the most visceral levels. I could feel Something, Someone, peeling away my skin, pulling me out as if I were a piece of marble being sculpted by a Master Sculptor. Chip by chip, this Sculptor was drawing out the real me—to reveal his vision of the masterpiece inside.

Before I knew it, I had my hands in the air and my eyes turned heavenward as my praises rose in sweet communion with God's Spirit. I sang with all my heart: "How great thou art! How great thou art!"[1]

In those moments, I became a new creation. Maybe I hadn't been blinded like Paul or struck dumb like Zechariah, but in that instant, I knew who was in charge of my life and who held the source of my true power. I knew, too, that all the restless energy that had been building inside was God's energy, a powder keg of explosive potential that had been stored up for one purpose only: to glorify him. My life, my art, wasn't mine at all; it was God's, and I gave it up to him that very moment.

I barely waited for the preacher's invitation. The minute the minister opened his mouth, I jumped to my feet and ran down to the front of the auditorium to rededicate my life to Christ. As I knelt at the steps of the altar, the floodgates opened, and tears of joy and thankfulness poured out.

⟳

I didn't have all the answers then, and I still don't. I was just a twenty-two-year-old kid who wanted to create paintings for a living. The odds seemed impossible, and yet I knew with complete assurance there was only one way to overcome the obstacles before me. I had committed my life to God, and then two weeks after my conversion, I trusted him to act.

---

[1] "How Great Thou Art." © Copyright 1953 S. K. Hine. Assigned to Manna Music, Inc., 35255 Brooten Road, Pacific City, OR 97135. Renewed 1981 by Manna Music, Inc. All Rights Reserved. Used by Permission. (ASCAP)

God, I need you to be my art agent, I prayed. *Open the doors you want me to walk through, and slam shut the doors that will lead me down the wrong path.*

But if I had any expectation of seeing miracles immediately, I was wrong. God, in his infinite creativity, had a more humble path in mind—at least for the moment. A few weeks after graduating from art school, after years of chafing to experience life at its most real, my friend Jim and I had a flash of divine inspiration:

Jim looked at me, and I looked at him, and we said, "Let's hit the road." As I've mentioned earlier, that trip riding the rails from coast to coast set me on a creative course that mushroomed into an artistic career that has spanned more than twenty-five years. A year after returning to California with Jim, I was showing my original landscapes and western scenes in galleries throughout California. By the following year, I had married Nanette and we were selling prints of my paintings in front of the local shopping center, where we took the first tentative steps toward sharing my vision of being the "Painter of Light."

With God as my agent, I was free—free to make my life and my art a worshipful expression of my love for him.

Perhaps you're ready to experience your own version of "radical faith." You may not see yourself speeding down a freeway on a Harley or shouting hallelujahs at the top of your lungs at a revival meeting. But you may be ready to trust your life to God totally, without worrying what tomorrow may bring. You may be ready in your heart to lift your drooping hands and strengthen your weak knees in order to be healed once and for all of the doubts and the fears that keep you from realizing your creative potential spiritually.

Start making your entire life an act of worship—right now. You just might discover that God will become your agent, too. One thing is certain: The mighty hand that created the universe in all its splendor is more than capable of shaping your private world into a thing of incalculable beauty and wonder.

THE PRINCE OF PEACE

Window on Another World

In perhaps its most powerful expressions, worship is filled with hope—hope that there is indeed some sovereign power beyond us who cares . . . hope that life will have a happy ending . . . hope that we may be healed or transformed.

In the end, worship is about God, not about us. Many of us have moments of profound recognition, flashes of divine insight when we recognize that a supernatural power has broken through our daily lives to give us a glimpse of the eternal. Those moments often come when we least expect them. We may be walking down a gritty street or riding in a crowded bus, and all of a sudden we see the people and the world around us the way God sees them, through eyes of total love.

After the moment passes, we might slip back into our ordinary routines—taking the kids to Little League, or getting groceries, or doing our taxes, or having a sales meeting. But the memory is imbedded in our spirits as an everlasting touchstone, a reminder of the joy and peace at hand.

For some of us, though, God breaks through in such a powerful way that there is no slipping back into "ordinary routines." One person who has experienced such a breakthrough is Jeanne Murtaugh, a fifty-year-old executive in Greensboro, North Carolina. Jeanne survived a bout with breast cancer back in 1991, only to be diagnosed with cancer again eight years later. The week before her second surgery, Jeanne had to undergo a battery of tests—brain scans, bone scans, a GI series—and she was scared.

"I don't handle tests well," she confessed, "and so before my first test,

I started to pray." Inadvertently, she found herself softly singing part of Handel's *Messiah*.

"Wonderful, Counsellor, The Mighty God, The Everlasting Father, The Prince of Peace," she sang to herself.

Before long her prayer became more specific, as over and over she repeated, "Prince of Peace, bring me peace; Prince of Peace, bring me peace."

For three days in a row, she repeated that prayer before each test, not knowing why or how it had come into her mind. The following Saturday, just days before her surgery, Jeanne flew to Boston to celebrate a client's retirement, and during a free afternoon, she wandered around the marketplace at Faneuil Hall. There along the main street, she spied a little art shop. Although she had never been to one of our Thomas Kinkade Galleries, something drew her inside.

Jeanne was wandering from room to room, looking at cityscapes, such as my newly published *Pike Place Market, Seattle,* and western landscapes, such as *Lakeside Hideaway,* when she heard a male voice echoing through the gallery.

"It's unbelievable," he said. "It's incredible."

Wanting to know what all the fuss was about—and being "naturally nosy," Jeanne followed the voice to an office in back of the gallery. Poking her head inside, she saw the owner of the voice talking to a woman behind a desk. He was pointing to a painting on the wall—a simple portrait of Jesus' downcast head, painted in broad brushstrokes against a pinkish-brown background. The painting stopped Jeanne short.

"It was so different from everything else in the gallery that I couldn't help asking, 'Which artist is this?' "

"Why, Thomas Kinkade," said the woman behind the desk. "It's one of his early works."

Brushing past the desk, Jeanne walked boldly up to the artwork to see the piece more closely. When she saw the inscription, she let out a little gasp of recognition.

"*The Prince of Peace: A Portrait of Christ,* 1980." As it turned out, my impressionistic portrait of Jesus, which I had painted when I was an art student in my early twenties, had just been released as a print and hadn't yet been exhibited on the gallery floor.

Jeanne was awestruck. "I thought back to my prayers earlier in the week and my upcoming surgery. With all of the tests I had undergone during the past eight years, never had I prayed to God as 'Prince of Peace.' Those words just hadn't been in my vocabulary. And yet, only days before seeing this painting, I had heard Handel in my head and repeated 'Prince of Peace.' What was even more astonishing was that there was no reason I should have been singing words from the *Messiah*. It wasn't even Christmas—it was October."

As she pondered the painting, Jeanne was overcome with a deep sense of assurance. "This peace was a promise of how I should approach the journey I was about to take," she said. "God had put me right where I needed to be—in front of this painting, at that moment in time."

Since the gallery's only copy of the print was already committed, Jeanne flew home to North Carolina and bought a copy at the Kinkade Gallery in her hometown. The day before her surgery, she hung it on the wall in her great room, and for the next ten months, through tortuous rounds of chemo and radiation, she lay on the couch meditating on the painting and praising God, the Prince of Peace.

"Thomas Kinkade could have given that painting any number of names," said Jeanne. "But it was as though he had painted that painting more than twenty years ago just for me."

Today, Jeanne is free of cancer. But the promise—and hope—expressed in that painting continues to remind her each and every day of her life that *now* is the moment to worship. *Now* is the time to celebrate the gift of health and the love of family and friends.

This story and many like it are a reminder to me that whatever talents each of us might possess are in the end not all that important. What matters most is how the God of the universe can use each of us—you, me, even Michelangelo—to touch another life in an unforeseen way.

STREAMS OF LIVING WATER

A Call to Worship

 n the final analysis, worship itself is a creative act. In its purest form, it is a total outpouring of our true selves—our creative selves—to the One who made us.

The supreme challenge for each of us is to find ways to transform our daily experiences into an ongoing creative journey, a never-ending exercise in bringing glory to our Creator. Those who can learn to discern the presence of God in the minutiae of an occupational routine or daily labor—whether carpooling kids to school or choreographing a Broadway show—will discover a great treasure that will illuminate every corner of their lives. In short, they will discover the spirit of worship.

It all comes down to a matter of choice: How will you use the creative talents within you? Will you belittle the gifts you've been given, regarding them as "frivolous" and relegating them to an obscure corner of your life? Will you use them to tear down those around you, by pandering to popular taste and culture? Or will you use them to uplift and inspire others, by infusing everything you do with meaning and purpose?

As a painter, I've had to ask myself such questions throughout my life. Also, to find my own beliefs about the true meaning of my art, I've had to sort through a morass of conflicting views. I encounter some who think of art as mere decoration, something to fill a space over the couch or brighten up that little nook in the corner. To their way of thinking, artists are those who can put colors and shapes together in pleasing configurations. In this view, creative types are primarily those who have learned the techniques for conveying on canvas lovely images that we hold dear: a restful seascape, a mountain vista, or even a formal portrait of Mom. But this approach to art has never satisfied me.

I know others for whom art is a form of protest, a challenge to the status quo employing raging, clashing forms and grotesque images as a means to memorialize pain and man's inhumanity to man. Such people view artists as agitators, thorns in the flesh of society who are destined to sound a universal call to arms. They celebrate Picasso's *Guernica,* with its distorted bodies, angry-eyed creatures, and sharp-edged black-and-white contours, as a portrait of raw evil enshrined on the wall. At the sight of it, their stomachs tighten and they recoil in horror, shrinking under the weight of terrifying darkness. And though I certainly respect such creative impulses, these views don't resonate completely with my own.

In the end, after years of painting and reflection on the meaning of my work, I've concluded that art is akin to worship. It is the highest form of human expression, a form of prayer. In the creative act, there is a merging of mind and body that engages God's Spirit and activates mysterious forces within to direct us toward our highest purpose.

In fact, from the day I saw the light pouring out of that picture of the Golden Gate Bridge in the gallery on Fisherman's Wharf with my father, I sensed instinctively that art was something transcendent. To me, it was positive, pure, powerful, and peaceful, all rolled into one. It was holy.

As I have grown older, I have come to believe that in an expansive sense, creativity is God's highest calling, our highest human imitation of our Father. And I have come to believe that he has set us all apart to use our imaginations for his purposes. I create because it's my purpose in life; it's what God has destined me to do, whether through my paintings, my family life, or my work with various charities. He has set me apart to try my best, using whatever talents and energy I may possess, to bring light out of darkness and to let my light shine before men. He has set me apart to worship him through every ounce of my creativity—to act as a reflector of his awesome goodness—and in so doing even to guide others to that perfect light, his light.

The same is true for you. You, too, have been called to be a light-bearer and to express through your creativity a sense of awe and wonder at God's majesty. This call to creativity isn't complicated. It could be as simple as telling your child a fanciful story at bedtime, or as difficult as diving deep within yourself to forgive someone who has hurt you. It could be a life's work or a ministry for the moment. Whatever your occupation or daily responsibilities, once you discover your special creative calling and begin to fill in life's canvas, you'll be on the way not only to a profound experience of worship, but also to an experience of creative living that is your own work of art.

And believe me . . . in God's perfect timing, it will be a masterpiece.

A New Day Dawning

Behold, a New Thing

You have moved through seven days of creative living, from solitude . . . to passion . . . to true love . . . to community . . . to joyful work . . . to conflict . . . and finally to worship. But what's next?

In the spirit of the prophet quoted at the beginning of this book, it's now time to experience a "new thing" in your life—a permanent, personal transformation that can make every day a creative masterpiece. But it won't do simply to read my words and nod your assent in the abstract. Rather, your personal challenge is to find a way to make every one of the seven days described in the previous pages *a vital, ongoing reality* in your very heart and soul. This means each of us must somehow find a way to make creativity a part of our everyday existence.

Of course, there are a number of paths you might take to reach this final destination of a life permeated by the creative impulse. But one simple approach that has worked for me and others is to set aside some quiet, solitary time each day, preferably the first thing every morning, to meditate on the personal meaning of each of the days we have explored in this book.

For example, you might spend a minute or two reflecting on the importance of finding opportunities for solitude in your busy schedule. Then you could devote another minute or so to pondering possible ways of infusing your life with more passion . . . and so on. As you go through each creative day in your imagination, allow new ideas or pictures to float in and out of your mind.

When I'm musing in this fashion, I find it quite helpful to keep a journal and a pen near at hand so that I can record what I experience. Otherwise, I'm likely to forget fleeting thoughts and insights. It's also helpful to assume an active, interactive stance during this exercise. In other words, you might frame specific concerns and needs that occur to you in the form of specific questions about each creative day. Here are some suggestions:

On solitude: "How do I need to organize my life *today* to provide myself with more time alone for creative thinking?"

On passion: "What is my single, most important passion in life— and what will I do *today* to release that passion in creative activity?"

On true love: "What are the most important love relationships in my life—and what can I do to improve them—*today*?"

On your community: "What creative contributions can I make to my community *today*—even if those contributions represent only small steps forward?"

On your job: "How can I transform those seemingly humdrum tasks that face me at work *today* into an exciting array of creative challenges?"

On conflict: "What conflicts do I anticipate in my life *today,* and what's the best way for me to manage them efficiently and creatively, while not allowing worry or frustration into the process?"

On worship: "What steps do I need to take *today* to make the experience of worship an integral part of my daily life—and not just an occasional activity?"

After posing each question to yourself, sit silently for a few moments and reflect on possible answers. When thoughts drift into your mind, record them on the paper in front of you. Then move on to the next question.

This period of creative rumination is also an ideal time for prayer. For example, as you ask yourself each of the above questions—or other questions of your own choosing—you might redirect your thinking to a broader spiritual plane by asking, "God, will you show me the answer to this question?" Or you might even pray proactively, "God, please empower me to love the unlovable people in my life."

This entire process should take only ten to fifteen minutes. But at the end of the session, you should feel spiritually, emotionally—and physically—rejuvenated with a greater sense that you are becoming more centered or focused on the most important things in life.

True creativity, after all, cannot be contained in a conceptual box or compartmentalized in one easily controlled segment of our lives. Instead, authentic creativity is often explosive, unpredictable, or even unruly by human standards, as it emanates through mysterious channels from the Greatest Creator of them all.

So as you reflect back on what you have read in this book, and perhaps spend some time meditating each day on what creativity means in your life, it's important to keep in mind that there can be no end to the true creative process. Certainly, you can—and should!—delve ever more deeply into your chosen art form or other creative activity. But you can never hope to "arrive" or to comprehend it all.

Every creative day is a new day, which will be built to some degree with old skills and upon previous insights, but which also must move beyond the old and encompass that which is totally fresh and innovative. That's why I always find it helpful to keep the words of the prophet at the forefront of my mind as I prepare to create: "Remember not the former things . . . Behold, I am doing a new thing; now it springs forth, do you not perceive it?"

Yes, Lord, do a new thing now in the lives of each of us who earnestly seek *The Art of Creative Living*.

Amen, and amen.

Selected References

Bartlett, John. *Familiar Quotations.* Christopher Morley, ed. Boston: Little, Brown and Company, 1951.

Elsen, Albert E. *Purposes of Art.* 2nd ed. New York: Holt, Rinehart, and Winston, 1967.

Guptill, Arthur L. *Norman Rockwell Illustrator.* New York: Watson-Guptill, 1946, 1975.

King, Stephen. *On Writing.* New York: Scribner, 2000.

Larkin, Oliver W. *Daumier: Man of His Time.* New York: McGraw-Hill, 1966.

Mankowitz, Wolf. *Dickens of London.* New York: Macmillan, 1976, 1977.

Rickenbacker, Edward V. *Rickenbacker.* Englewood Cliffs, NJ: Prentice-Hall, 1967.

Rockwell, Norman. *Norman Rockwell: My Adventures as an Illustrator.* New York: Harry N. Abrams, 1988.

Tolkien, J. R. R. *The Hobbit.* Boston: Houghton Mifflin, 1966.

Wright, William Aldis, ed. *The Complete Works of William Shakespeare.* Garden City, NY: Garden City Books, Doubleday, 1936.